Learn to play Guitar

A comprehensive guide for beginners to intermediate players

By Gareth Evans

ISBN   978-0-9569547-0-1

Written and Published by Gareth Evans

Photography, Diagrams and Cover design by Gareth Evans

Additional Illustrations by Chris Evans

Copyright © 2011 by Gareth Evans

Audio Tracks

These can be downloaded for free from **www.intuition-books.com**

1	Canon in A	(Demo)	22	Bayou Noir	(Backing)
2	Canon in A	(Backing)	23	Florida Blues	(Demo)
3	Basic Blues	(Demo)	24	Florida Blues	(Backing)
4	Basic Blues	(Backing 80bpm)	25	Root and Fifth	(Demo)
5	Basic Blues	(Backing 90bpm)	26	Root and Fifth	(Backing)
6	Calm Beach	(Demo)	27	Power Arpeggio	(Demo)
7	Calm Beach	(Backing)	28	Power Arpeggio	(Backing)
8	Summer	(Demo)	29	The Bikers…	(Demo)
9	Summer	(Backing)	30	The Bikers…	(Backing)
10	Nice	(Demo)	31	Heavy D	(Demo)
11	Nice	(Backing)	32	Heavy D	(Backing)
12	Over the Hills…	(Demo)	33	Travelling Man	(Demo)
13	Over the Hills…	(Backing)	34	Travelling Man	(Backing)
14	Route 5	(Demo)	35	Boogie Boy	(Demo)
15	Route 5	(Backing)	36	Boogie Boy	(Backing)
16	Mosey on Down	(Demo)	37	B Minor Blues	(Demo)
17	Mosey on Down	(Backing)	38	B Minor Blues	(Backing)
18	Headstrong	(Demo)	39	Improvising Exercise 1	
19	Headstrong	(Backing)	40	Improvising Exercise 2	
20	Motown riff	(Demo)	41	Improvising Exercise 3	
21	Bayou Noir	(Demo)	42	Improvising Exercise 4	

Introduction

This book is designed for beginners to intermediate players. It explains in a simple way the fundamentals of areas such as technique, theory, and fret-board layout, some of which you are better off knowing now, rather than after a few months, or even years of playing.

Depending on your experience some of the subjects, particularly earlier on, may already be familiar although there may be something you have missed and whatever your strengths are there might be other areas to be brought up to speed. This book looks at technique in some depth.

Music theory is reinforced by musical pieces in various styles, which should make the learning process more practical and enjoyable. The pieces are designed for beginners but can be adapted by more experienced players by making their own melodies and / or improvising using the scales.

Each audio track has two versions, a demo track to show how the piece should sound, followed by a backing track where the guitar has been removed for you to play over.

Stretching is particularly important in the earlier stages as the hands are more prone to injury and annoying pains before they have got used to playing. At the back of the book (Chapter 7) are some stretching exercises and tips on how to practise. You don't need to wait until you have finished the book to read that section as the advice can be useful from the beginning.

Contents

Chapter 4 - Playing by Shapes

Chapter 5 - Reading Rhythm

Chapter 6 - Further Techniques

Chapter 7 - Tips

The Guitar

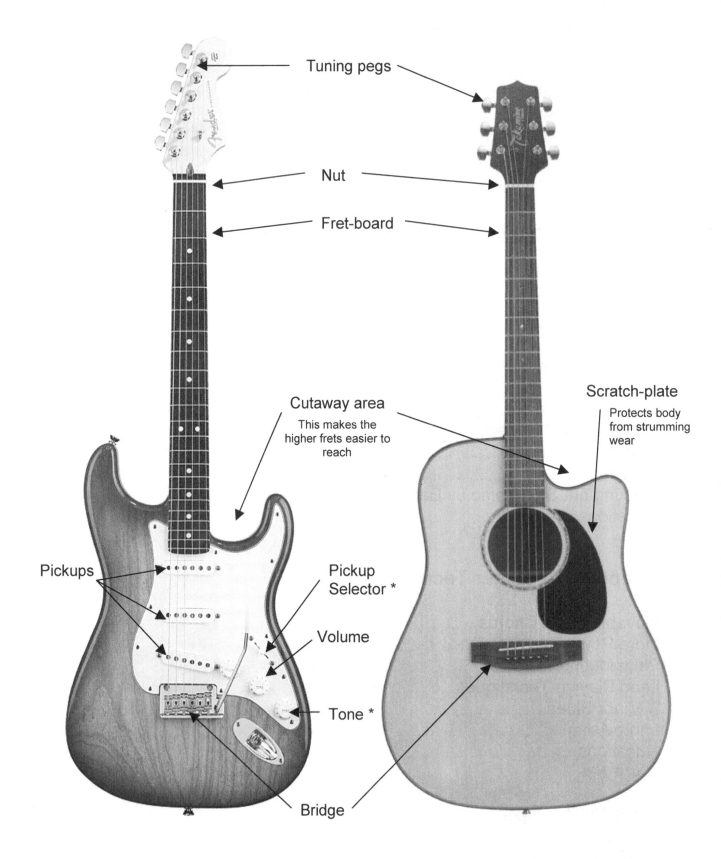

Tuning pegs

Nut

Fret-board

Cutaway area
This makes the
higher frets easier to
reach

Scratch-plate

Protects body
from strumming
wear

Pickups

Pickup
Selector *

Volume

Tone *

Bridge

* The Pickup selector switch is to choose which pickups to use. Ranging from a sharp heavy sound with the switch back for the pickup near the bridge, to a softer mellow jazzy sound with the switch set forward for the pickup near the fret-board.

* The Tone knob controls the volume proportion between the high and low frequencies, in other words it's the treble and bass.

Basic Technique…Holding the Guitar and using a Pick

When sitting to play the guitar you should be upright with the guitar upright on your lap and its neck tilted upward slightly. It can help to have the guitar as balanced on the lap as you can, as this leaves the hands free to play it rather than have to hold it upright too.

With an acoustic guitar you can hold the body of the guitar under your strumming arm. Using a music stand at eye level for reading can make it easier to maintain good posture and is more comfortable than crouching over your guitar to read music off a table or desk. Pegs can be used to hold pages open.

Sometimes when standing up to play, the guitar is slung low, usually for style. For the best position to play in however, it's better not to have the guitar slung too low otherwise it becomes difficult for your fretting hand to reach around the neck. Wearing a strap while sitting can also give extra stability and comfort.

The pick should be held between the thumb and the index finger. The parts in contact with the pick should be the sole / tip area of the thumb and the side of the sole of the index finger. You could put your hand out in front of you and hold the pick as shown in the photo.

There only needs to be a small bit of pick sticking out from your grip. Too far out and we don't have as much control causing it to flap about within our grip as we pluck the strings.

When writing we hold the pen nearer the tip while resting the side of our hand on the paper, this way we can get control over the pen and write neatly. If we were to hold the pen further away from the tip without resting our hand on the paper our writing could look pretty messy!

Similar applies to using a plectrum. Unless you are strumming it is best to rest your hand on the guitar, this way you can get more control and accurately play the strings you intend to…

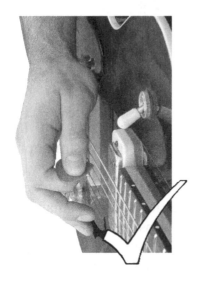

On the picture to the left the "wrist / muscle at the base of the thumb" area is resting on the guitar. Use this technique.

On the right the hand is hovering over the guitar. This isn't very easy to control and makes it likely you will accidentally play strings that you didn't intend to.

When playing the higher strings the hand moves down and the wrist / muscle at the base of the thumb area rests on the lower strings. This mutes the lower strings when we don't want them to sound. It also maintains the same posture for the hand across all six strings rather than bending the wrist down and stretching the fingers to reach the higher ones.

If you have a movable bridge try not to rest the hand on it and move it while you are playing.

Some players like to have the remaining fingers tucked in, others like to have them fanned out. To get more control when playing the higher strings you could also rest the little finger on the guitar just below the high E string.

The metal bars on the guitar neck are frets. You push the string down just behind these with fingers from your fretting hand to get different notes when the string is plucked by the other hand. Avoid bending the string up or down as you press so that the note doesn't go out of tune. If the string makes a buzzing noise then you might need to press down a little harder.

Having said that you shouldn't press *too* hard either because whether you press quite hard or just hard enough the note will still be clear! You can find out by pressing a finger very lightly on a fret while plucking the string, gradually increase the pressure until you hear a clear note, that's all the pressure you need. If you practise like this so it becomes how you play, then eventually you'll move around the fret-board easier without your fretting hand getting tired.

Try this on various strings and frets using all fingers from the index to the little finger (and don't forget to use the technique from the last section for the hand that plucks the strings). You'll probably find the little finger more difficult than the rest but don't worry, as this is something that can be worked on over time.

Tuning the Guitar

First we need to understand the strings of the guitar. They are named according to what note they sound when played open. Open means a string is played on its own without the fretting hand pressing down on any of the frets.

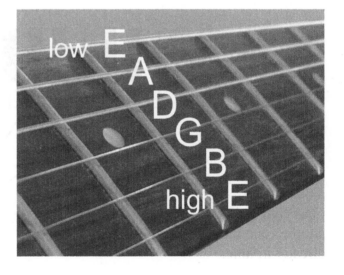

Even though the low E string is positioned on top of all the other strings it is the lowest in pitch, which is why it is called the "low E" or "bottom E", while the string that is physically below the other strings is the highest in pitch hence its name "high E" or "top E". To make the string names easier to remember a mnemonic can be used such as "Every Angry Dog Grows Big Ears". The strings can also be named numerically from the high E to the low E as the 1st, 2nd, 3rd, 4th, 5th, and 6th string.

There are a number of ways to tune a guitar. The easiest and most accurate is with an electronic tuner. An Electronic tuner can be plugged directly into the guitar. Most also have an internal microphone so they can be used to tune an acoustic guitar too.

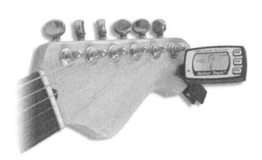

Another kind of electronic tuner is the clip-on tuner, which reads vibrations from the instrument. Distraction from other sounds will be minimal compared to using a microphone tuner. A clip-on tuner can be used for electric guitar or acoustic guitar, wherever the clip will fit.

Using a tuner is accurate and good for situations like exams or performances. Another way is to tune the guitar by ear, which can develop your sound perception. Below is how you would refer to the keys of an in tune piano or electronic keyboard to tune a guitar.

Listen to the note played on the piano while tuning the corresponding guitar string so that it sounds the same...

You could also tune your guitar to another one that is already in tune.

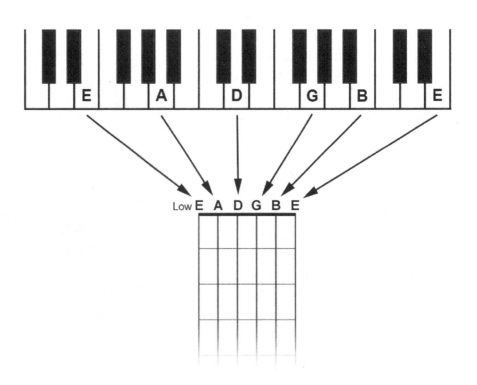

Relative Tuning

Finally, the well-known relative tuning method, which shows how the strings relate to each other.

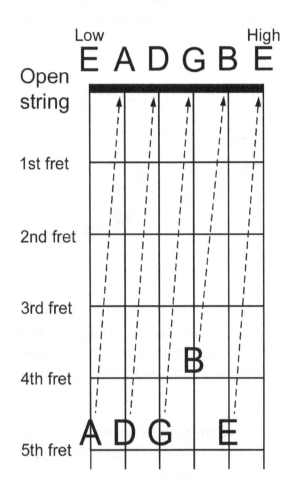

When you play the 5th fret of most of the strings, it gives the same note as the next string up played open. The diagram to the right shows how this works. Providing that the low E string is in tune, we can play its 5th fret to give us the note of A and tune the open A string so it sounds the same. Once the A string is in tune, its 5th fret can then be used to tune the D string. You can work your way up through the strings tuning them in the same way.

The only exception to this method is the B string. Rather than being tuned to the 5th fret of the G string it needs to be tuned to the 4th fret of this string. The different tuning of the B string will play an important role in a later section of this book (pages 66 to 69) so it's worth bearing in mind.

A potential problem with the relative tuning method is that the margin of human error might be times six by the time you have got to the high E string, so you would need good ears.

One last thing worth considering with tuning in general is that when a string is plucked, initially its pitch tends to rise slightly, this is particularly true for the lower strings. If you use an electronic tuner and pluck one of these strings reasonably hard then let it ring, you might notice after a second or two the dial of the tuner settles down a bit to the actual pitch of the string.

Tablature

Tablature or "Tab" for short is a simple way of reading for the guitar as it gives a graphical representation of the fret-board. The six horizontal lines represent the six strings of the guitar with the high E string at the top and the low E string at the bottom. The following diagram lines a guitar up next to some tablature to show this…

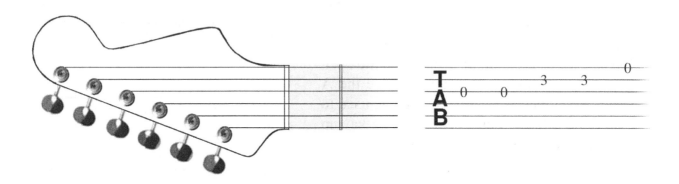

The numbers on the strings tell us what fret to play on, or if the string is to be played open when there is a "0". The above TAB is telling us to play the open G string twice then the 3rd fret of the B string twice, followed by an open high E string.

If you are wondering why it's "upside down" this is so that it matches conventional notation (explained later) which places higher pitched notes toward the top line and lower pitched notes toward the bottom line, hence for tablature the high E string at the top and the low E string at the bottom to match. Another reason could be because when you look at the guitar on your lap while playing it, the high E string is in the "top" of your field of vision because you are looking downward!

Here is a simple piece to play to get an idea of reading from tablature...

When the fret numbers are vertically aligned they are played at the same time, which gives a chord. Here's a simple sequence with three basic chords…

It is also important to consider what fingers we are using. The picture shows how the fingers of the fretting hand are numbered.

Below is the same melody with numbers added underneath to indicate what fingers should be used on the frets…

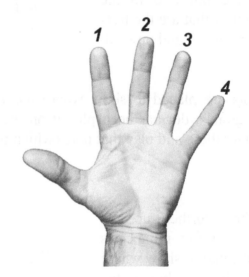

The finger numbers happen to be the same as the fret numbers for this piece as we are playing at the bottom of the fret-board. Further on in the book these numbers have been added where necessary to indicate what fingers should be used on which frets.

13

Fret-board Diagrams

These are used to show scales or chords and can be either horizontal or vertical. Similar to tablature they give a graphical representation of the fret-board. In the diagram below, the horizontal lines represent the strings, which are shown the same way around as the tablature. The thicker vertical line on the left is the nut and to the right of that are the frets from the 1st and upward.

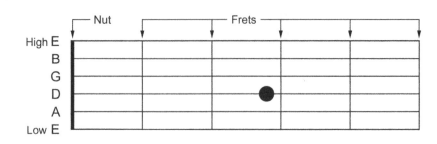

Dots are placed to show where the fretting fingers should be placed. In the above diagram a dot has been placed on the third fret of the D string so you would place a finger there and play that note (which is F).

When further up the neck, a fret number is indicated to show where on the fret-board the diagram is located. On the diagram to the right you would play the 6th fret of the D string (which is the note of G♯)

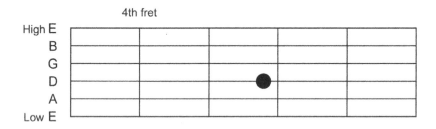

Vertical fret-board diagrams are often used for chords as they don't usually span across as many frets as scales.

On the example the strings are arranged as shown across the bottom. The nut is now at the top (where the thicker line is) while the frets are below. The easy version of a C major chord is shown. Numbers have been added next to each dot to tell us which fretting fingers to use. The "O" above a string means to play that string open and an "X" above a string means that string is not played, so for this chord you would strum from the D string to the high E string.

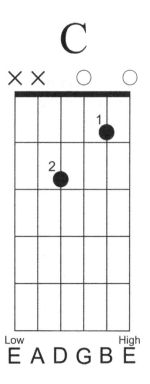

14

Sight-reading ...a brief introduction

Although tablature is easy to understand and we can learn a piece of music from it relatively quickly, it doesn't tell us anything about rhythm. Conventional music notation on the other hand tells us about both pitch *and* rhythm. This is a basic introduction to notation so at this stage you don't have to sight-read. Later on in the book (page 79) the rhythmical aspect of notation will be covered so that you can use it in conjunction with tablature.

Conventional music notation is written on the five line *Staff* and is often included above tablature. In the example below, the notation and tablature both represent the same guitar part. Both the staff and tablature are divided into bars, which are separated by bar lines.

Guitar music is written in the *treble* clef 𝄞 which is at the start of the staff. The numbers just to the right of the clef, one on top of the other, are the *time signature*, which tells us about the pulse of the music; i.e. how we would count it.

The five horizontal lines of the staff don't represent strings in the way that tablature does. They are like a chart that tells us the pitch of the notes. The higher the note is placed on the staff the higher in pitch it is, and the lower the note is placed the lower in pitch it is. When notes are so high or low that they go outside of the staff, *ledger lines* are used to extend the staff, such as on the 2nd, 3rd and 4th bars of the example.

Whether the stem of any note points upward or downward is simply to make the staff look neat depending where the note is placed. The higher the note the stem goes down such as on the first two bars of the example, while the lower the note the stem goes up such as on the second two bars of the example.

> **Note:** Although from now on in the book conventional notation will be included above all tablatures, you don't have to read from it until later on when it is further explained.

Canon in A 1&2

Playing notes at the bottom of the fret-board can be difficult at first because you are pushing down near to where the strings are held up by the nut (you can see where the nut is on page 6).

The following short piece is written with this in mind. It is based on the song "Canon in D" by Johann Pachelbel. Play the notes that you see in the tablature. The letters above are the chords to accompany it, don't worry about these. Numbers have been added underneath to help with the rhythm, which you would count "One Two Three Four". Play the notes where the numbers are circled in black; so that's on *One* and *Three*. At the bottom of the page is some help with finding what frets to play…

This is a repeat sign, when you get to it go back to the beginning and repeat. For this piece repeat four times (as indicated by the "x4").

The first three notes are easy to find as they are on dotted frets.

Jingle Bells

For this simple version of Jingle Bells numbers have also been added underneath to help with the rhythm. Straight from beginning to the end, no repeats.

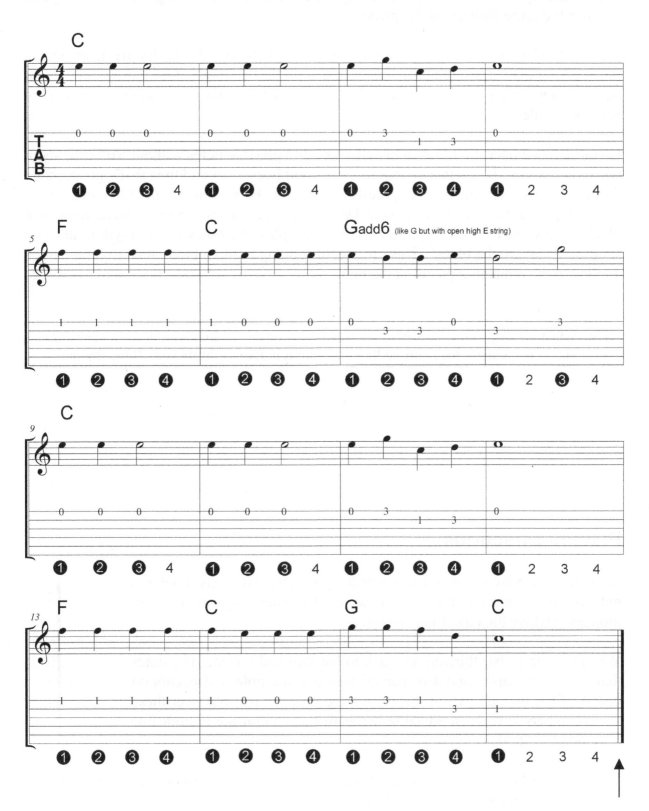

A thin and thick line with no dots indicates the end of a piece.

Let's play some blues. Over the page is a simple blues melody that uses notes from one of the most popular scales for guitarists, the *minor pentatonic* (more on this later). Numbers have been added under the Tab for the first few bars to help with the rhythm and as before the ones circled in black are when the notes occur. The notes on beats 3 and 4 lead up to the note on the stronger beat 1 of the following bar. This rhythm remains the same throughout the piece.

This method is used in various places in the book to put the scales we learn into a musical context. The melodies written are a guide but if you feel more confident or have already been playing a while, feel free to make up your own melody or improvise using the scales.

If you're a beginner, first look at the tablature and play the notes without worrying about when they occur. If you can do that to the second line or beyond then that's great, that's the melody (the second line is hardest). Next, for the rhythm count *"One Two Three Four One Two Three Four One Two Three"* etc and clap or tap your guitar where the black circles occur. Once you have done that, play the notes to the rhythm and you should be playing the blues! This process of looking at the melody then rhythm can be applied to the remaining pieces in the book.

Tip: When playing to the backing track watch out for the 3rd line, you need to concentrate on counting particularly hard here so that the drum roll doesn't throw you off the rhythm.

Playing Directions

For Canon in A we came across a repeat sign. Basic Blues uses one too but also has a corresponding sign facing the other way on bar two, indicating where the repeat is to begin.

When you finish bar thirteen, go back to bar two and repeat. The notes that occur on beats 3 and 4 of bar thirteen and the note that occurs on beat 1 of bar two are part of the same three note phrase split over these bars (numbers have been added underneath the Tab on the bottom line also to help with that).

Once you get back to bar 13 again, this time around continue to the final bar where the piece finishes on the 3rd fret of the high E string.

Basic Blues

🔘 3, 4 & 5

Remember to use corresponding fingers across as many frets i.e. the 3rd finger for notes on the 3rd fret and 2nd finger for notes on the 2nd fret.

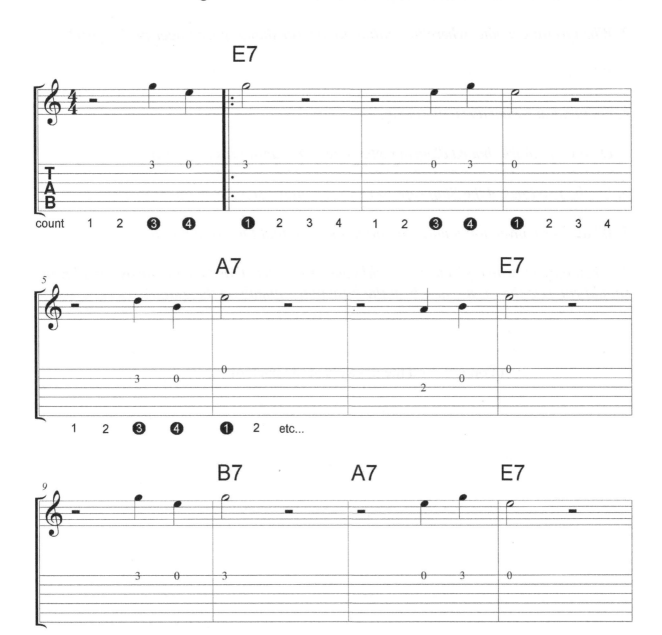

Note: The chords on this piece (like A7 and E7) are to accompany the melodies and are on the backing tracks. You don't have to play these.

That's the end of the first chapter here are a few questions...

1. *Which string is tuned differently from the rest?*

2. *When fretting a note, where in relation to the fret should your finger push down?*

3. *Why is tablature "upside down"?*

4. *On tablature what does "0" mean?*

5. *On a vertical fret-board diagram what does "X" above a string mean?*

6. *Do the five lines of the Staff represent strings in the same way tablature does?*

7. *What does conventional music notation indicate that tablature doesn't?*

8. *When playing with a plectrum should your arm hover above the guitar as you play or should you rest the wrist / muscle at the base of the thumb on the guitar?*

(You will find the answers at the back of the book)

Fret-board Layout

There are twelve notes in music, as follows…

1	2	3	4	5	6	7	8	9	10	11	12
A	A# B♭	B	C	C# D♭	D	D# E♭	E	F	F# G♭	G	G# A♭

The diagram to the right shows how the notes are arranged across the A string as they go up its frets. At the 12th fret we return to the note of A but at a higher pitch, this is known as an *octave.* If we were to continue above the 12th fret to the 13th and upward, the sequence of notes would repeat in a higher octave A# / B♭, B, C etc…

Like the chart we can see that B and C are next to each other as are E and F. All of the other notes are two frets apart with a flat or sharp note in between (signified with # for sharp and ♭ for flat). These are different names for the same note, also known as *enharmonic equivalents.*

This is similar to how the keys of a piano are laid out. Below is a diagram that shows a section of the piano. The notes go across the keys in a linear fashion similar to a single string of the guitar. There are also octaves on the piano, so if you go up (or down) the keys eventually you end up on the same note but at a higher (or lower) pitch, a couple are marked out on the diagram…

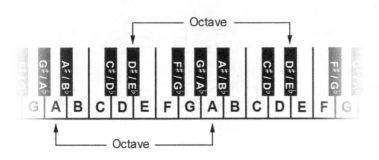

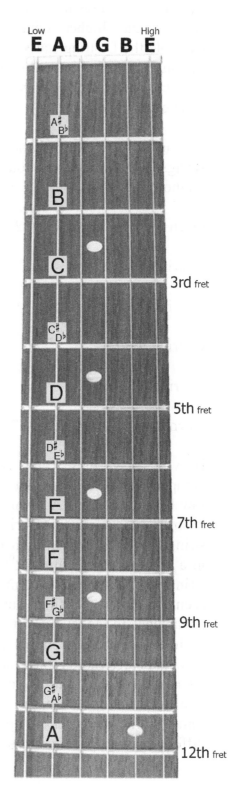

The guitar has six strings however! Over the page, another diagram shows the notes of all six strings of the guitar up to the 12th fret…

Before we go any further, it's worth pointing out that the idea of this section is to learn how the fret-board is laid out. You're not expected to learn all the notes at this stage.

Starting with the note of the open string the musical alphabet goes up the frets of each of the strings until at the 12th fret it reaches the higher octave. So for example the D string starts on D, goes up the musical alphabet until on the 12th fret it reaches the note of D again in a higher octave.

The notes occur several times over all six strings. For example the note of E occurs on the...

Open low E string and its 12th fret

A string 7th fret

D string 2nd fret

G string 9th fret

B string 5th fret

Open high E string and its 12th fret.

If you play those and listen while comparing, you'll hear that the 12th fret low E string, 7th fret A string and 2nd fret D string are the same. G string 9th fret, B string 5th fret and open high E string are in a higher octave while 12th fret high E string is a higher octave again. This may seem complex at first but there are advantages to the layout of the fret-board such as transposing shapes by the root note and barre chords (these are explained later in the book), and as you can't play more than one note on any string at the same time, in order to play chords, different strings need to be used.

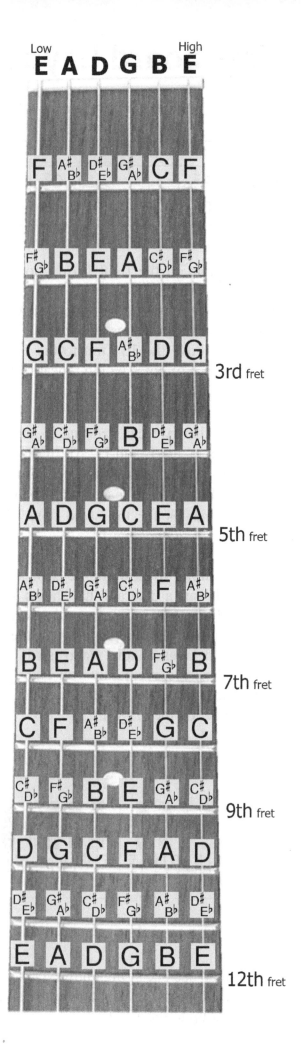

22

The Major Scale

Tones and Semitones

In Western music there are two fundamental distances between notes, these are the *Tone* and the *Semitone*. On the guitar a tone is two frets apart while a semitone is one fret apart, both can be in either direction back or forth…

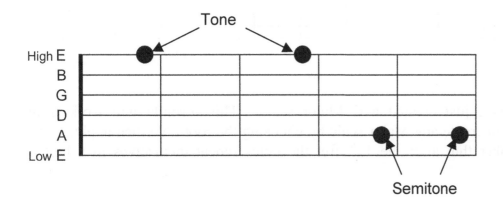

It doesn't matter where you are on the fret-board tone and semitone, are always the same.

Sequences of tones and semitones are used to make scales, and the first and most important scale we'll be looking at is the Major scale. The Major scale is the basis of music in the West. Everything else in Western music is defined in comparison to it. Scales may seem boring at first but knowing them, particularly this one, opens up doorways to understanding many other aspects of music. The Major scale consists of seven notes, their distance from each other measured in tones and semitones. This gives us numbers known as *intervals,* which relate to how far the notes are from the starting note (the root). As follows…

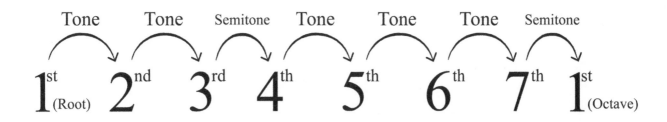

The formula takes us to the higher octave of the root note. An easier way to remember the scale is that there are tones between all of the intervals except for between the 3rd and 4th and between the 7th and the octave, which have a semitone between them. The full names for these intervals are the *major 2nd, major 3rd, perfect 4th, perfect 5th, major 6th and major 7th*. The 4th and 5th are known as *perfect* because they are neither major nor minor. Scales are usually indicated with numbers like the above diagram, so the Major scale could be represented simply as 1 2 3 4 5 6 7.

Let's create a Major scale on the guitar. Start with the 1st fret of the B string giving us the note of C. This will be the root note of our Major scale. From this root note move up the fret board according to the formula **TTSTTTS** and we should end up with a completed Major scale...

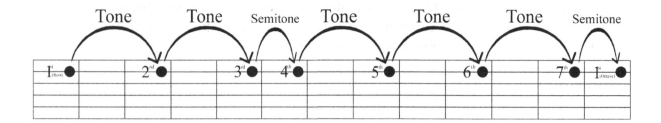

Well done you have just created a C Major scale. This formula will work from anywhere so we can create any Major scale by choosing the root note then applying the formula. Remember that after the 12th fret the notes repeat themselves in a higher octave.

Using the fret-board diagram from the last section we can see what the notes are of any Major scale that we make (including the C Major we have just made). More on that soon, in the meantime there is a musical piece on the next page based on an E Major scale with its root note on the open high E string...

Note: The Tone and Semitone can also be referred to as the "Wholetone" and "Halftone" but it's easier to say TTSTTTS (and therefore perhaps remember) than WWHWWWH.

Calm Beach 6&7

There are four beats per bar, the notes you play are on beats *two* and *three*. This is the same for all the bars. If you find locating some of the frets difficult remember the notes are all from the single string E major scale.

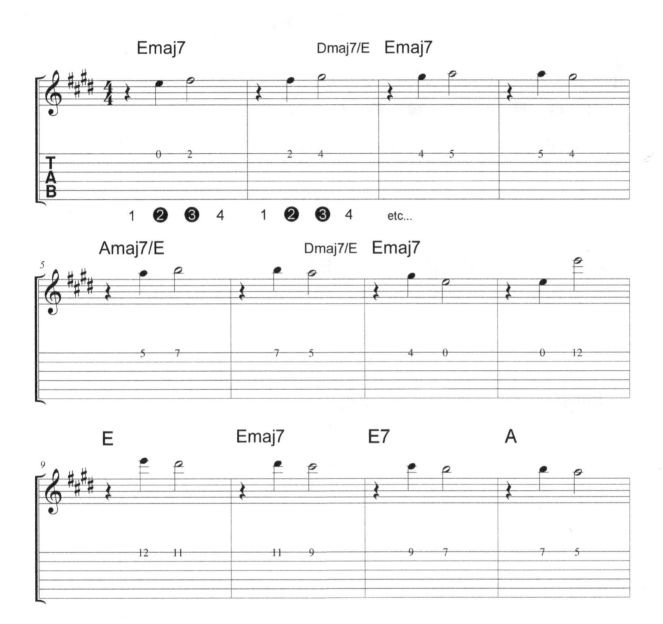

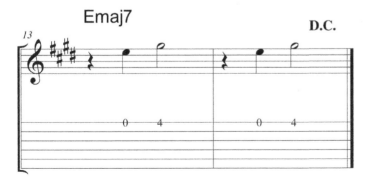

D.C. stands for *Da capo* meaning "from the beginning", so you go back to the start and play through the piece again finishing on the last bar.

Here's a blank Tab to pencil in your own version if you like. To keep it simple the five line Staff has been taken off. Use notes from the same E major scale across the high E string and keep the rhythm the same, playing on beats two and three for all the bars. Use your ears, what sounds best?...

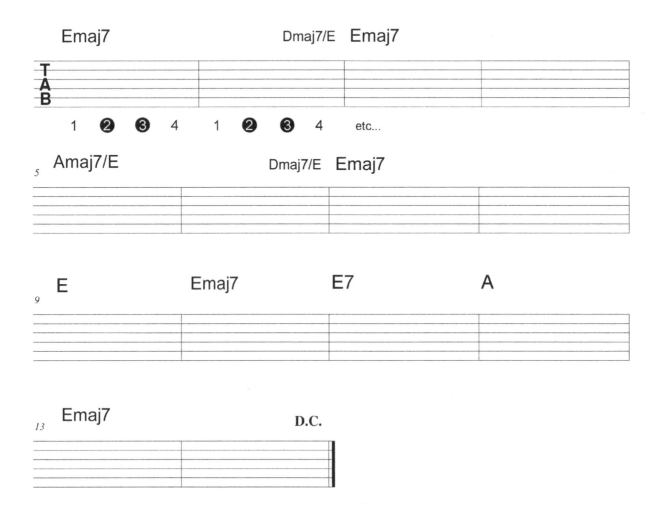

Notes in the Major Scale

As mentioned earlier on page 24 we can use the fret-board diagram to see what the notes are of any major scale that we make. To the right a D major scale is highlighted on the fret-board diagram. The notes of the D major scale are…

D E F♯ G A B C♯ D

The reason two of the notes are known as sharps, is because this keeps it alphabetical. If we had called those notes flats then the letters G and D would both have occurred twice as $G^♭$ then G and $D^♭$ then D.

Why not work some out for yourself on the diagram? Choose a root note near the nut then work your way up the frets of the string according to the Major scale formula (Tone, Tone, Semitone, Tone, Tone, Tone, Semitone)

If you start on the 1st fret of the high E string to give us an F major scale, is the 4th interval (on the 6th fret) best known as B flat or A sharp?

What are the notes of the C major scale from earlier?

What are the notes of the E major scale that we used for the "Calm Beach" piece, and are the notes that fall on enharmonic equivalents better known as sharps or flats?

The major scale across one string gives a visual representation of how far the notes are from each other and is similar to the way the scale would be played across the keys of a piano. However, so that we don't have to move up and down the guitar's neck, a version that goes across different strings is used. This will be covered later.

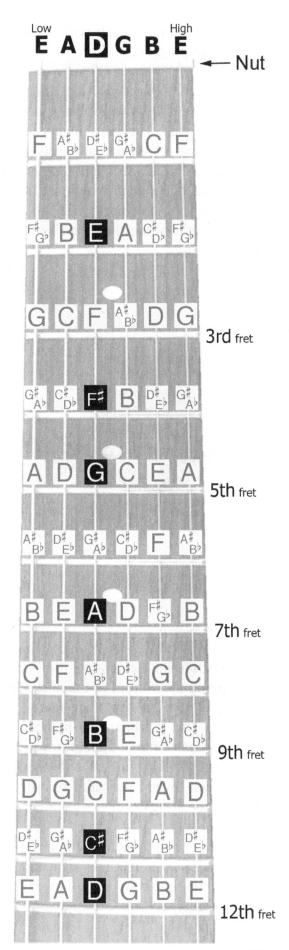

Fretting Hand Technique

Now that we have dealt with some basics it's time to look in more detail at techniques needed to progress further.

Photos **1** and **2** show good position for the fretting hand. The four fingers are spread out to reach across as many frets, while the thumb behind the neck is roughly central to the opposing fingers, which are at about a right angle to the neck. The tips of the fingers rather than the "pads" press down on the strings…

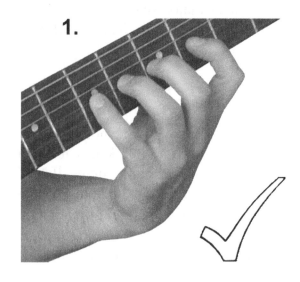

1.

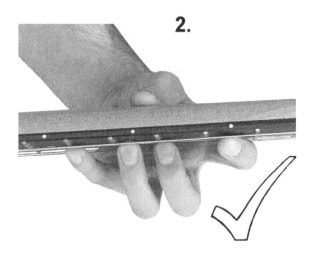

2.

The only parts of the hand that should be in contact with the guitar are the fingertips on the fret-board and the "pad" of the thumb behind on the neck. This posture also makes it easier to shift up and down the neck.

Photos **3** and **4** (4 over the page) demonstrate bad technique. In 3 the palm is hugging the bottom of the neck while the thumb is over the top. The fingers are too close to the fret-board to manoeuvre and the hand can't move up and down the neck very easily. The fingers will also have to bend back toward the palm in order to fret the higher strings.

There are exceptions to the thumb position. For example, sometimes it can help to anchor the thumb over the top of the neck for stability if you are playing a string bend.

3.

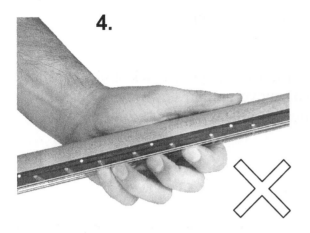

4.

In 4 the thumb isn't positioned centrally to the fingers as it rests behind the neck. Instead it's resting flat and is past the index finger, making it harder for the 3rd and the little finger to reach higher frets.

Poor technique can be due to the hand having not developed enough strength and shouldn't become a habit.

Alternate Picking

It can be tempting to do what feels natural and to some this might mean only picking with a downward motion. However in order to get to the next downward pick you have to move the plectrum back up to get into position anyway! So why not use this upward motion to pick as well and increase the efficiency and potential speed that you can play?

Let's start by picking the D string down and up to give a repeating D note. This is best done to a metronome so that you can practise getting an even tempo...

Down   Up

 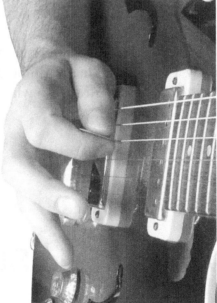

In the pictures notice how the angle of the pick changes slightly as I pick down and up.

Although the pick should be held firmly, it needs to tilt very slightly within your grip as it rolls off the string, so don't hold it too rigidly.

If the skin around the part of your thumb and index finger that is holding the pick turns a shade of white, then you're probably holding it too tightly.

Below is an exercise for alternate picking that goes through all six strings.

The arches ⊓ and points V represent downward and upward pick strokes. Arches for downward and points for upward. As you move up and down the strings try to maintain the same posture in the hand as mentioned earlier on page 8…

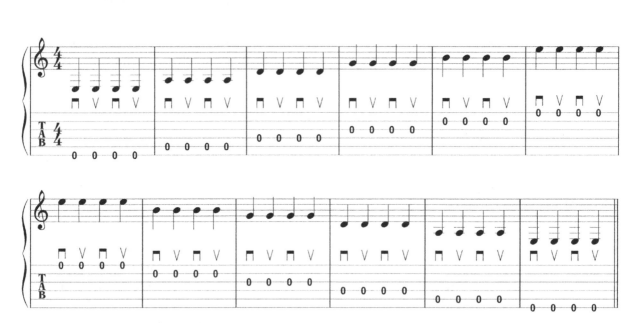

If the arches and points don't seem to make sense, it might be worth noting that these symbols originate from the different ends of a violin bow. The arch is for the blunt end near where the bow is held, which moves towards the floor when pulling the bow down. The point is for the pointed end of the bow, which moves upwards when pushing the bow up. Seeing as the downward motions are usually on a stronger beat it might help to remember it by how the arch is more substantial and blocky looking.

A simple part you could play to get used to alternate picking is the original Formula 1 theme tune "The Chain" by Fleetwood Mac. Although the part does vary it starts off with a repeating E note (the open high E string) so why not have a go?

Major Scale Shape

As mentioned earlier the major scale across a single string gives a visual representation of how far the notes are from each other. Now let's play it across different strings so that we can keep the hand in the same position, not having to move up and down the neck.

Below left, a C major scale has been highlighted. To its right is a fret-board diagram of the same scale played across different strings and at the bottom of the page it's in tablature to show how you would play it…

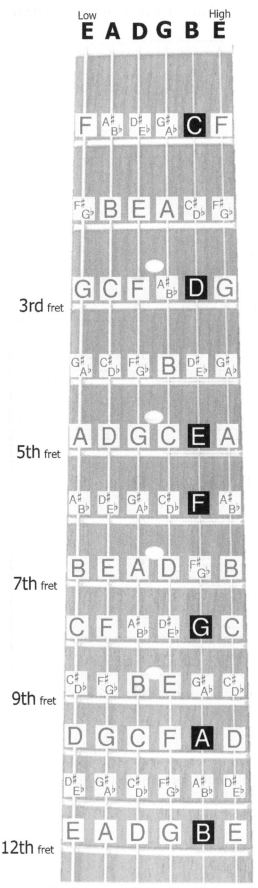

The last note of C major (C) is on the 13th fret of the B string.

3rd fret

As it uses a smaller area of the fret-board the above diagram only needs to go to the 3rd fret. The new scale shape is an octave lower with its root note (C) on the 3rd fret of the A string, this is because if you started from C on the 1st fret of the B string there wouldn't be enough strings to complete the scale.

Here it is in tablature with alternate picking directions and numbers underneath for the fretting fingers…

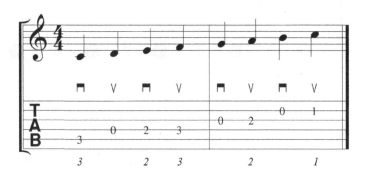

Over the page is a laid-back pop melody using this C major scale...

31

Summer 8&9

This piece uses a first and second ending; Once you have played to the repeat sign on bar 8, go back to the beginning and repeat, but this time, skip bar 8 and go to bar 9 then continue from there to the end of the piece.

Remember the melodies written are a guide, but if you feel more confident feel free to make up your own melody or improvise using the scale.

The Natural Minor Scale

Here we'll see how the Major scale can be altered to create a natural minor scale. Let's look at the original Major scale formula again...

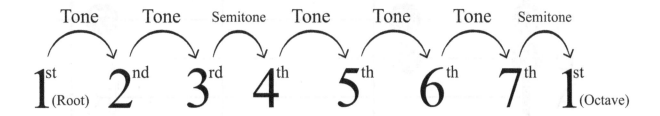

For the natural minor scale the 3rd, 6th and 7th intervals are lowered by a semitone and are now called the minor 3rd, minor 6th and minor 7th. In the scale formula this semitone lowering is indicated with the use of the flat symbol ♭ (this is different from note names such as "G♭ or E♭" so don't get them confused). The natural minor scale is as follows...

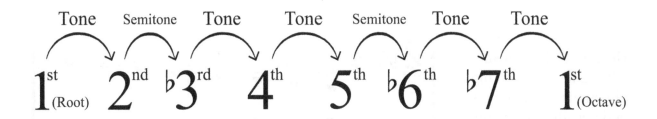

Here is the C Major scale from page 31 with these intervals lowered (the "R" symbols signify the Root note and its higher octave)...

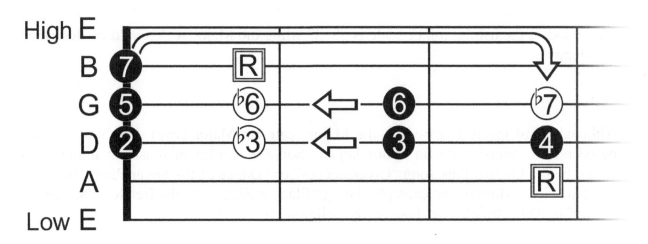

The minor 3rd and minor 6th are fairly simple as they are one fret lower. To lower the 7th you can't get any lower on the B string than the open B itself so the minor 7th has been placed on the 3rd fret of the G string. The result over the page...

Giving us a C minor scale…

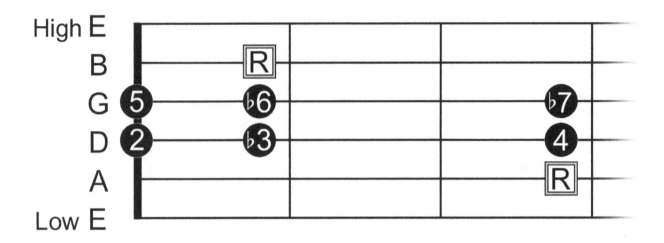

The notes of the C minor scale are: C D E♭ F G A♭ B♭ C (you could check and compare on the fret-board diagram at the top right of page 31).

Here it is in tablature with alternate picking directions and numbers underneath for the fretting fingers…

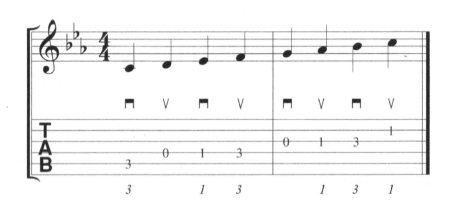

The mood of the natural minor scale is "Sad" while the Major scale could be described as "Happy".

Although most music is based on the Major scale (in Major keys) there's also much based on the minor scale (in minor keys). Some examples of music in minor keys would be the English Folk song "Greensleeves" or "Dance of the Sugar Plum Fairy" by Tchaikovsky. More recent examples being "Eleanor Rigby" by the Beatles, "Sultans of Swing" by Dire-straights or "Losing my Religion" by REM.

Over the page is a Jazz style melody using this C minor scale…

34

Nice 🔘 10 & 11

This piece uses D.C. (we first came across this for the piece "Calm beach" on page 25). It also has a repeat section. Play to bar 10 then repeat bars 9 and 10. After this go back to the start and play the piece again, but this time around, after repeating bars 9 and 10 continue to the end of the piece.

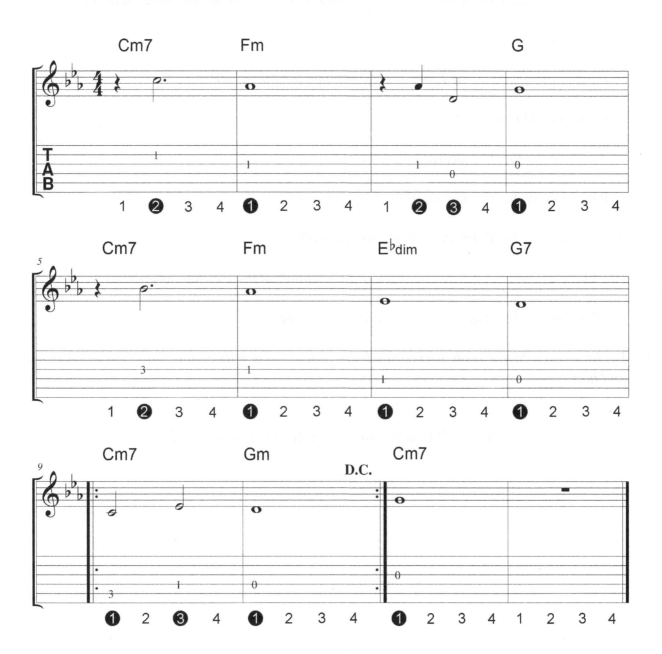

Chapter 2 Questions

1. *What is the term for a note that could be known as either a sharp (♯) or flat (♭)?*

2. *When going across the same string how many frets apart are the notes A and G?*

3. *When going across the same string how many frets apart are the notes E and F?*

4. *What is an octave?*

5. *What is the sequence of Tones and Semitones for the major scale?*

6. *What does D.C. mean?*

7. *What note is the 2ⁿᵈ interval of a C major scale?*

8. *What note is the 3ʳᵈ interval of an E major scale?*

9. *What note is the 6ᵗʰ interval of a D major scale?*

10. *Where behind the guitars neck should the thumb of the fretting hand be placed?*

11. *What do arches and downward points represent?*

12. *Between a Major scale and natural minor scale which three intervals are different and how?*

(You will find the answers at the back of the book)

Chords

Scales, such as the ones we have just looked at, are notes played in a sequence. Chords are notes played at the same time, and that's the main difference between them. Otherwise they are actually quite similar because chords are made up of intervals from scales.

Major Triads

The first and most basic principle behind chords is that we take the odd-numbered intervals from the scale. For the major triad, we take the root (1st), major 3rd and the perfect 5th from the major scale as follows…

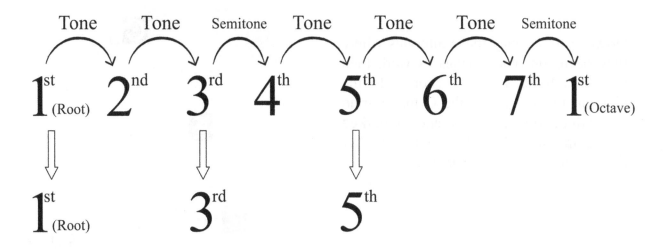

The fret board diagram below shows the C major scale from earlier with the 3rd and 5th marked out in white circles (the roots in squares as usual)…

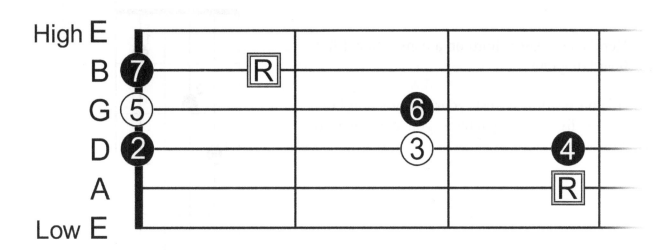

If we play these together we have a C major triad. In the photo the 3rd and 2nd fingers are used for the root (C) and 3rd (E) while the G string played open is the 5th interval. This major triad gives a clear major sound.

However if we play these intervals where they occur on other strings as well, then we get a fuller sounding chord. In the diagram to the right is the C major triad but with the root and 3rd (C and E) marked out again where they also occur in higher octaves on the top two strings...

Here's a C major chord on a conventional fret board diagram…

(If you need to refresh your memory on how to use fret-board diagrams you can refer to page 14).

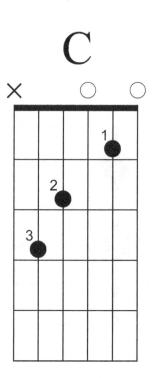

Major Triad Based Chords

Here are the shapes for the major chords in open position. Open position means they have open strings in them. The order the chords are shown reflects the name of the system used to keep them all in the same area of the fret-board, the C A G E D system…

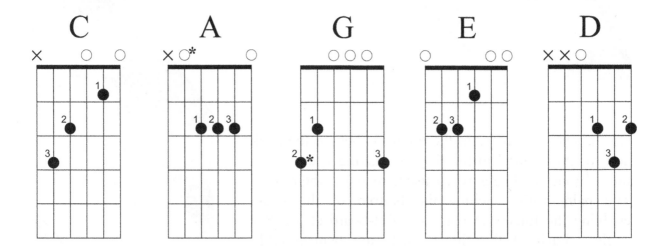

The chords are all named after their root note, and for these chords the root note is the lowest note. The root notes of the A major chord and the G major chord have been marked out with a * symbol. Can you find the roots of the E and D chords?

The four new chords look different to C major because the intervals are arranged differently within them. Like C major they're all made of the root, 3rd and 5th, for instance G major is made up of the root, 3rd and 5th from a G major scale. Although we have looked at where the intervals are located within a C major chord, as long as we know that these chords are based on the root, 3rd and 5th this is enough for now.

To make sure you are playing a chord as well as possible, play it one string at a time and listen to make sure each note sounds clear and isn't making any buzzing noise from a finger not placed correctly, not pressing down hard enough or accidentally touching another string.

> **Note:** This section is to learn the chords and get used to fretting them, strumming is covered in more detail on pages 42 then 50 onwards.

Over the page are a few more tips on technique…

The D major chord to the left is being played with bad technique. The palm is hugging the bottom of the neck and the thumb is over the top. The middle finger has to bend in on itself to reach the 2nd fret of the high E string. This technique doesn't make it easy to move up and down the fret-board.

On the photo to the right the thumb is behind the neck and roughly central to the fingers, making it easier for the 3rd (and 4th finger when used) to reach their frets. The palm isn't touching the bottom of the neck, enabling the fingers to reach the fret-board at a better angle. Each of the finger joints are bent roughly equally, just enough to make each finger curve around.

Maintaining this posture will help with all of the chords. These examples also illustrate use of the techniques mentioned in the "Fretting Hand Technique" section (page 28). Also, it helps to keep your fingernails reasonably short otherwise they might push against the fret-board before your fingers can.

If you have trouble fitting your fingers in for the A major chord, there's another way to play it using the 3rd or 2nd finger across the D, G and B strings (this is known as a "half barre"). If the note on the open high E string doesn't always sound, it's still an A major chord with its root, 3rd and 5th.

Minor Triads - To make a minor triad we take the root, minor 3rd and perfect 5th from the natural minor scale…

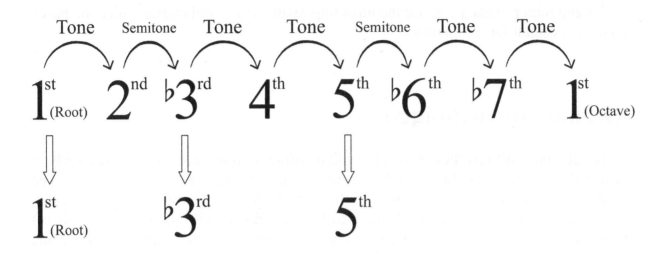

Another way of explaining the minor triad is that it's like a major triad but with a minor 3rd.

E   A   D

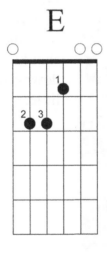 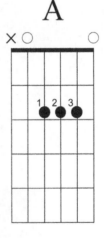 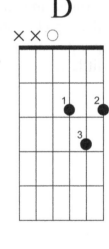

In the diagrams to the right some of the previous major triad based chord shapes have been placed above the new minor triad based chord shapes so that we can see the difference and therefore where the 3rd has been lowered...

Em   Am   Dm

Minor chords are indicated with a small "m" after the root note. Like the previous major chord shapes these also use their intervals more than once for a fuller sound.

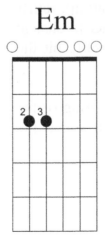 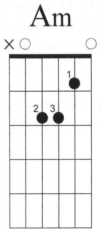 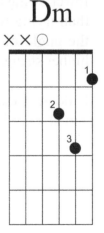

The original C major and G major open chord shapes have not been used to make minor chords as these versions are less practical for the fretting hand and they are not as commonly used. The shapes that have been used (E, A and D major) do convert easily to minor chords and are used more often.

Major and minor triads are by far the most important. They, and chords which are based on them, account for most music.

Strumming Technique

Although you don't rest the hand on the guitar, strumming is similar to alternate picking in that the plectrum should tilt slightly within your grip as it rolls off the strings. The harder you strum the firmer you need to hold the pick and maintain the correct angle. The angle of the wrist is as much dictated by the strings while the plectrum rolls off them, as you controlling your wrist. Try strumming up and down like this while keeping the wrist flexible and relaxed.

For downward strums the tip of the pick should point upward a little...

For upward strums the tip of the pick should point downward a little...

When strumming chords that don't use some of the lower strings (such as D major open position), rather than trying to miss those strings it's easier to change the angle of the strum so that you generally hit the higher strings.

It doesn't matter if you miss the lowest string of the actual chord occasionally, as it will still sound the chord.

Changing Between Chords

Now that we've learnt some chords let's look at how to change between them, as we would while strumming a song. It makes sense to change between different chords in the most efficient way. First, let's look at an example of a not so efficient way of doing this, changing from A major to A minor...

Starting with A major...   Changing to A minor…

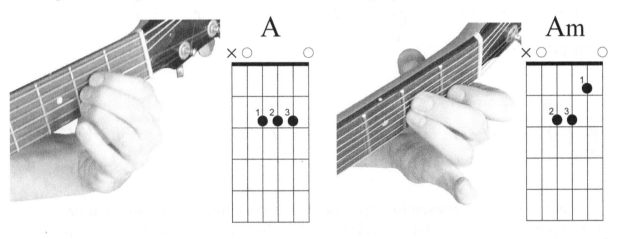

For A major the 1st, 2nd and 3rd fingers are used. Changing to A minor from this will mean all of these fingers have to come off their frets and reposition, but there is an easier way. The general idea behind changing between chords is to make the fingering of one chord as similar as possible to the fingering of the next chord so that there is as little movement as can be between them.

Here is another way of changing between A and A minor. For A major the 2nd, 3rd and 4th fingers are used instead while the 1st finger is kept behind on the 1st fret of the B string. This way, to change to A minor, all you have to do is lift the little finger off.

Starting with A major...   Changing to A minor…

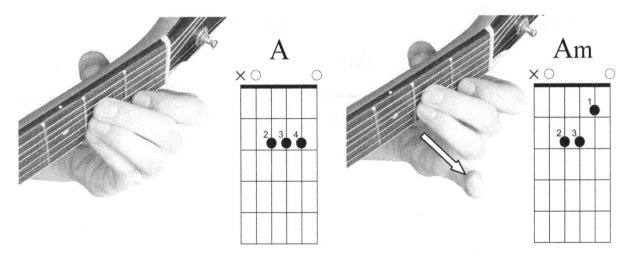

Move between A major and A minor like this a few times until you're comfortable with the change.

Now let's strum these chord changes in rhythm. For the following exercises the strumming has been kept simple with only downward strumming motion so we can focus on the chord changes while developing some basic co-ordination between the left and right hand. For these exercises the arch symbols previously used for alternate picking now apply to downward strums.

Each slash mark represents one beat and there are four beats per bar.

This and the following exercises are "x4" but if your fingers become tired or strained then it is best to rest for a bit as this is something that can be worked on over time. A to Am was a fairly easy chord change, the rest get progressively harder.

> **Tip:** It is best to use a metronome while doing these exercises at a speed you're comfortable with, then maybe a bit faster for a challenge. Remember the beat won't wait for you to change chord! so aim to get your chord changes good enough so that you can stay in time. If you find any of the exercises difficult you could try strumming only on beats one and three.

A minor to C Major

The 1st and 2nd fingers remain where they are on A minor while the 3rd finger moves from the 2nd fret of the G string to the 3rd fret of the A string.

From A minor…   to C major…

Move between the chords like this a few times until you're comfortable with the change, then try the following strumming exercise…

From C Major to E minor, then to A minor

First for between C and E minor, leave the 2nd finger where it is for both chords, take the 3rd finger off the fret-board and place the 1st finger on the 2nd fret of the A string.

From C major…   to E minor…

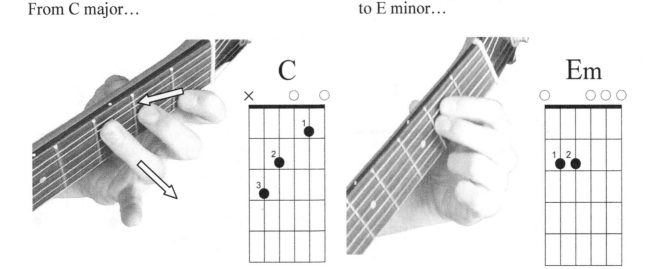

…then for A minor put the 3rd finger onto the 2nd fret of the G string and move the 1st finger back to the 1st fret of the B string.

to A minor…

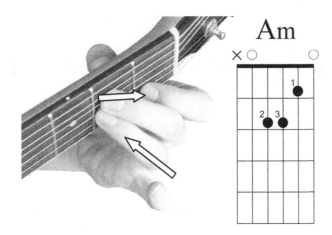

You might have noticed that the 2nd finger hasn't had to move at all throughout all three of these chords.

These three chords are similar to the sequence of chords used in David Bowie's "Space Oddity" song.

Move between the three chords like this a few times until you're comfortable with the changes, then try the following strumming exercise…

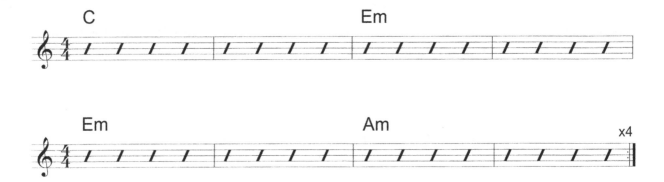

E minor to G Major

The 1st finger remains where it is for both chords, the 2nd finger goes to the 3rd fret of the low E string and the 3rd finger to the 3rd fret of the high E string.

E minor...   to G major...

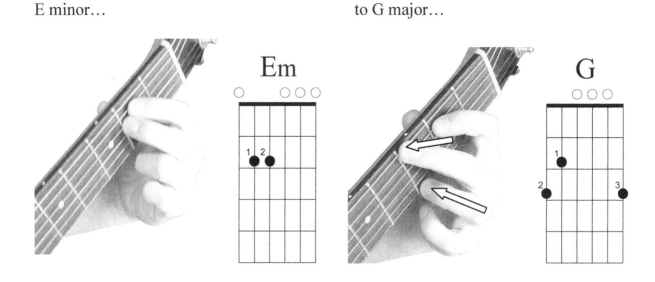

Move between the chords like this a few times until you're comfortable with the change, then try the following strumming exercise...

D Major to A Major

For this one the 3rd finger slides down the B string by one fret while the 1st and 2nd fingers are placed to give us the same fingering for the A major that was at the very beginning of this tutorial. It was not the best shape to move to A minor from, but for this example it is appropriate...

From D major...   to A major...

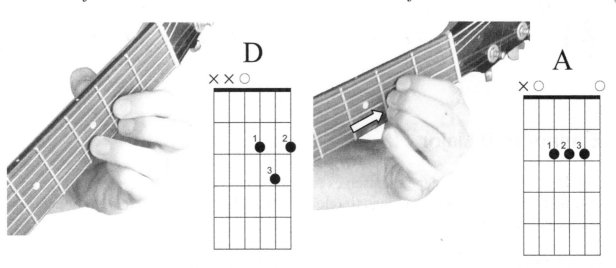

Move between the chords like this a few times until you're comfortable with the change, then try the following strumming exercise...

D Major to E Major

The 1st finger slides down the G string by one fret while the 2nd and 3rd swing around to place on the A and D strings for an E major chord...

From D major...   to E major...

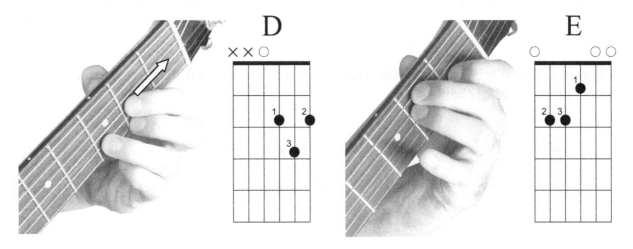

Move between the chords like this a few times until you're comfortable with the change, then try the following strumming exercise...

E minor to D Major

Not all chord sequences lend themselves to as efficient or easy changes. From E minor to D major has no simpler way than to relocate all the fingers no matter what fingers you use for either chord...

From E minor...   to D major...

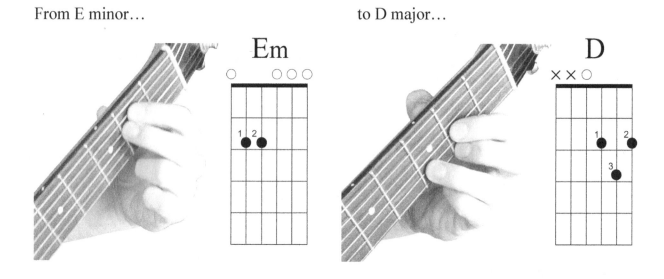

...and here is the exercise

Exercises 1 to 5 are similar to the previous one, so you need to move all the fretting fingers for the chord changes...

1.

2.

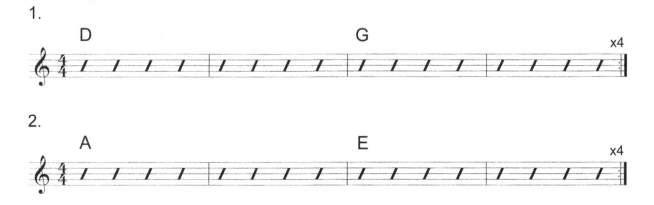

3.

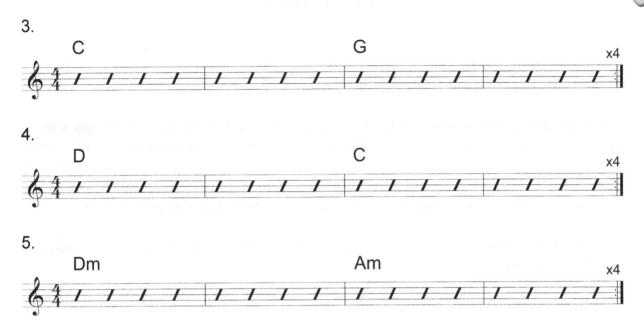

4.

5.

This chord progression has chords that can be fingered similarly *and* ones that can't.

6.

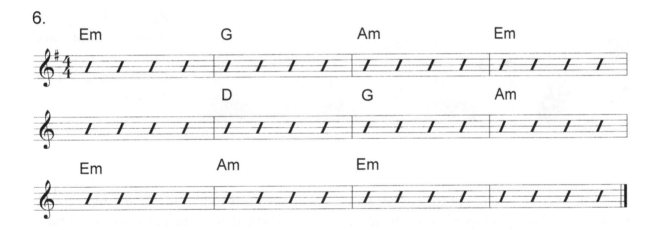

Always aim to have as little movement as you can between chords if possible. This general rule applies to all chord changes not just the ones used in this tutorial.

Strumming

It may seem logical to strum where the chords are, in fact that seems pretty obvious, however there is a bit more to it than that.

If the hand only moves when a chord is actually played then we don't have any way of measuring the time that's *in between* when we *aren't* playing, making it difficult to know when to come in when we *are* playing. The strumming hand should be moving down and up consistently with the beat *regardless* of when the chords are actually played. We will call the strumming movements in between chords *ghost strums*.

Let's look at a basic movement for this technique. We will need to count in groups of four beats, as follows…

One Two Three Four / One Two Three Four / One Two etc…

As we count, the strumming hand moves down and up on the beats as shown in the pictures below. Try this using only ghost strums at first so we can get used to the motion and rhythm, as this is the basic movement we will need for the forthcoming exercises.

One	Two	Three	Four

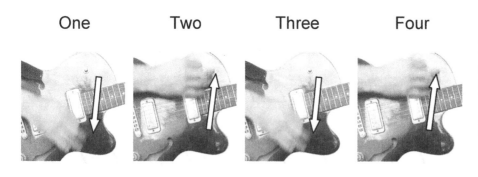

Repeat this, going straight from one bar to the next, i.e. 1 2 3 4 / 1 2 3 4 / 1 2 3 4 etc…

We will need only one chord leaving us free to focus on the rhythm. Something like E minor would be good as it's easy to fret and uses all six strings meaning we don't have to concentrate on avoiding certain strings while strumming the rhythms, although any chord that uses all six strings will do...

Em

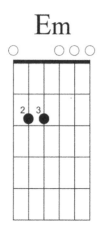

E

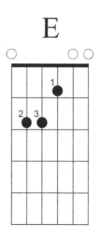

G

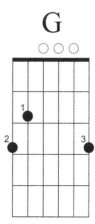

For the following exercises it helps to count out loud while you play. The beats written in bold capital letters indicate when you strum, the rest are ghost strums. Start with playing only on the first beat…

ONE   two   three   four

Repeat this, going straight from one bar to the next, i.e. **1** 2 3 4 / **1** 2 3 4 / **1** 2 3 4 etc…

Now play only on the second beat, which occurs on an upward strum…

one   **TWO**   three   four

Again repeat, going straight from one bar to the next, i.e. 1 **2** 3 4 / 1 **2** 3 4 / 1 **2** 3 4 etc…

Can you guess what's next? Yes, now play only on the third beat, which occurs on a downward strum…

one   two   **THREE**   four

Repeat this, 1 2 **3** 4 / 1 2 **3** 4 / 1 2 **3** 4 etc…

Finally play only on the fourth beat, occurring on an upward strum…

one   two   three   **FOUR**

1 2 3 **4** / 1 2 3 **4** / 1 2 3 **4** etc…

You may have found the second and fourth exercises a little harder because the strum was upward and came in on a weaker beat. The first and third are stronger beats.

Here's more of a challenge. All four of the previous exercises are played directly after each other, two bars of each. The arrows are to help guide you with the strumming, the larger black ones indicate when to play, and don't forget it helps to count out loud while you play…

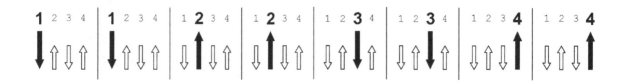

Try with only one bar for each…
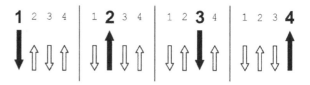

If you repeat the sequence the 4 at the end of the last and the 1 at the beginning of the next are right next to each other…

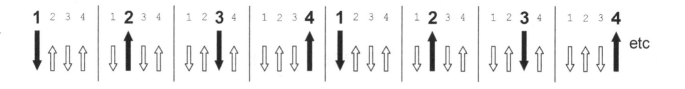

You could make up your own strumming patterns by choosing which of the four beats to strum on. Here are a few examples…

1.

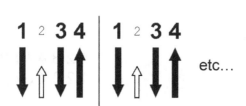

2.

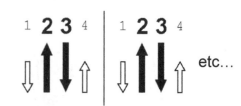

3.

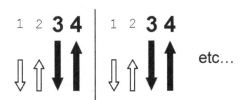

etc...

4.

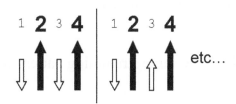

etc...

5.

Here's a pattern that goes over two bars...

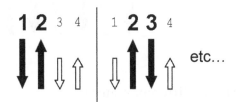

etc...

The better you get at this the more it starts to sound like the strumming you would have in a piece of music. So far we have limited ourselves to one chord. Most rhythm parts will have at least one chord change, so we need to learn how to co-ordinate our strumming hand and our fretting hand in order to strum while moving between various chords.

> **Note:** If you'd like to remind yourself on strumming technique, there are the tips on page 42.

Let's split each beat in half and count the point in-between with the word "**and**". So instead of "**One Two Three Four**" we now have "**One** *and* **Two** *and* **Three** *and* **Four** *and*". As before the strumming goes down and up but now we need to account for these halfway beats also, so the downward strums will occur on beats **One**, **Two**, **Three**, **Four** while the upward strums will occur on the "**ands**" in-between. As shown below...

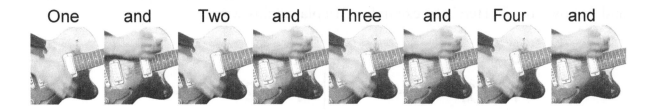

Have a go at counting that while moving your strumming hand accordingly. This is the underlying movement behind the exercises starting on the next page.

For the following three strumming patterns use one chord of your choice.

1a. The same strumming pattern over two bars…

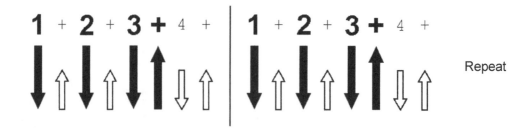

Repeat

1b. A different pattern…

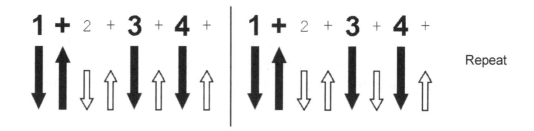

Repeat

1c. Here 1b and 1a are put together…

Repeat

Now let's play them with some different chords. For each exercise play C over bar 1 and Am over bar 2. Here's an example of 1a played this way…

Repeat

Try 1b and 1c like that also.

54

The next three strumming patterns are slightly more challenging. As before, try these with one chord only at first, then with a different chord over each bar, such as C for bar 1 and Am for bar 2 (like for the last set) or Em for bar 1 and C for bar 2…

2a. The same pattern over two bars…

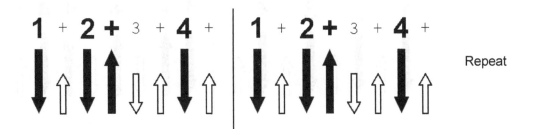

2b. A different pattern…

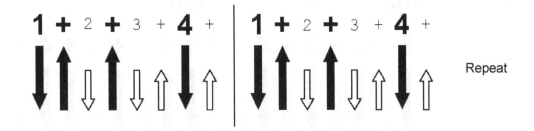

2c. 2a and 2b put together…

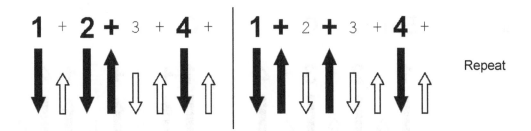

When we play on two upbeats or more in a row (such as for 2b) this is *Syncopation*. Here's a pattern that uses lots of syncopation…

2d.

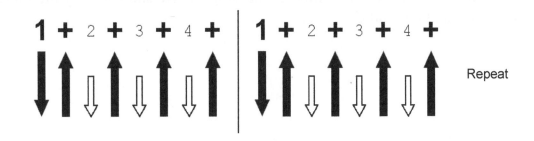

Now let's have some more chord changes. The following three exercises are the same strumming pattern over different sets of chords, starting with the easiest chord changes, ending with the hardest...

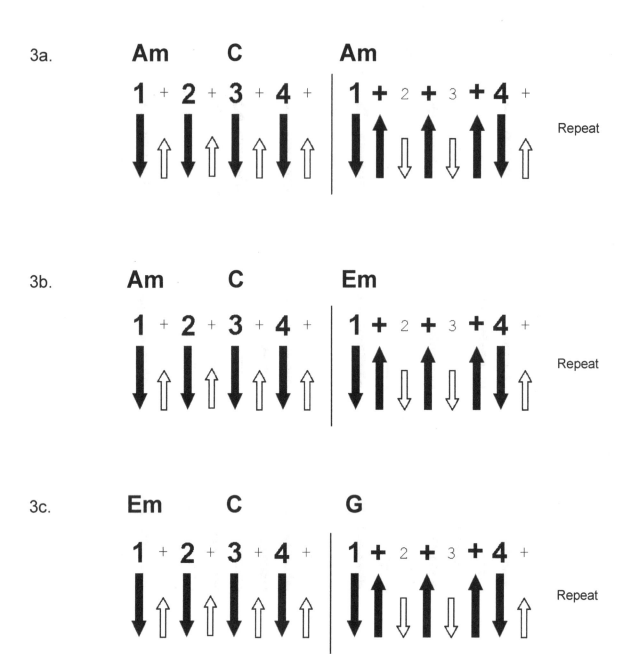

This strumming pattern is similar to the song "There she goes" by the La's, the chords of which are G, D and C.

Only two chords for the following but trickier to change between and the strumming pattern is a bit harder too…

4a.

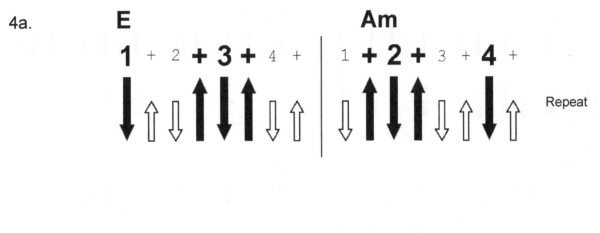

4b.

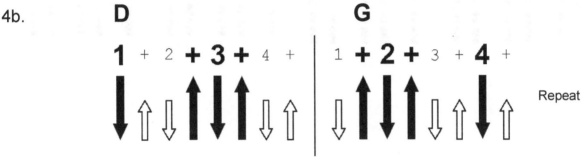

4c.

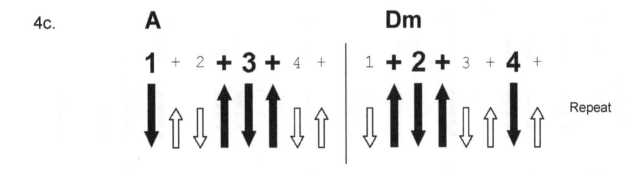

The next three strumming pieces (starting over the page) are sections from the same song. If you can play each of the three sections separately but not together as one piece this is fine, you could come back and try later when you are further on in the book. Count in the same way with "One and Two and Three and Four and".

5a.

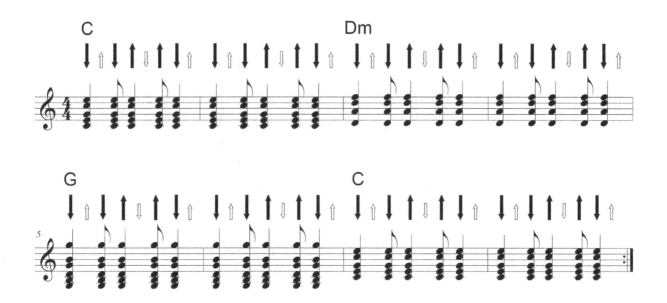

5b.

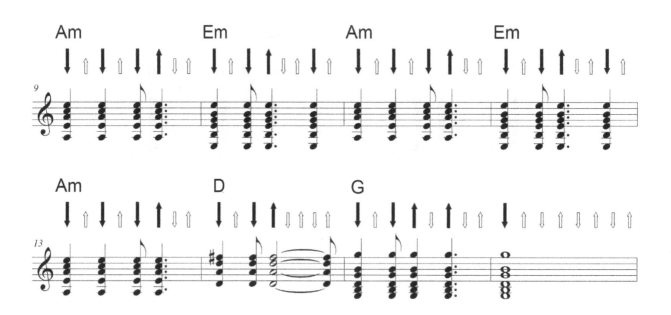

5c.

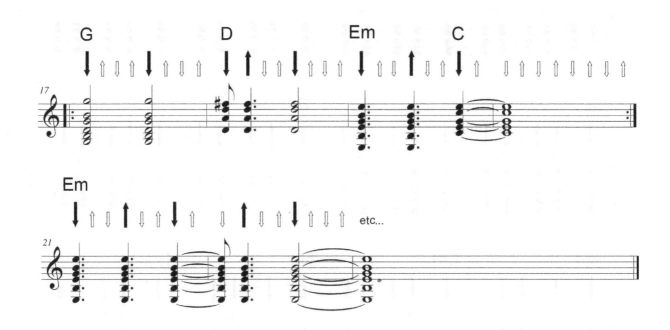

Over the page is the whole piece…

Over the Hills and Far Away

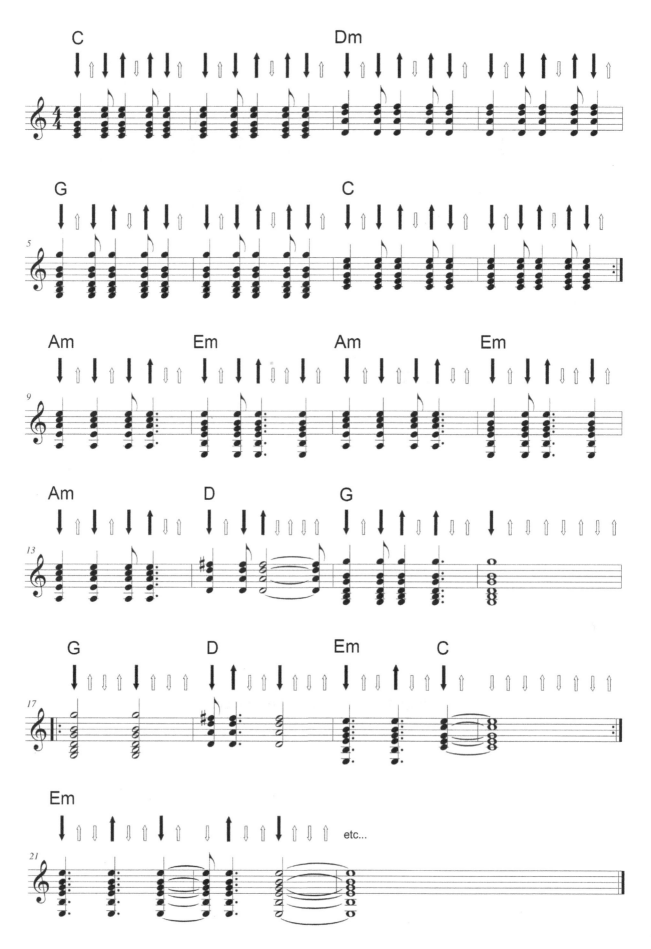

Chapter 3 Questions

1. *What three intervals are a major triad made of?*

2. *What three intervals are a minor triad made of?*

3. *The major and minor chord shapes are based on the major and minor triads but why do they contain more than three notes?*

4. *What is the root note of the chord D major?*

5. *What is the root note of the chord D minor?*

6. *What is the root note of the chord E minor?*

7. *What is the best way to change between chords and can this apply to all chord changes?*

8. *Why should the strumming hand keep moving when the chords are not being played?*

(You will find the answers at the back of the book)

Fretting Exercise

It can be tempting to use only the strongest fingers on the fret-board. However, if we learn to use all of the fingers we can play more efficiently and potentially faster. So far in this book we've hardly used the little finger.

The following exercises train each finger to move independently. They should be done to a metronome so that you can develop consistency in your technique and a sense of timing. Start slowly. On the next page is some advice on technique (Minimising Movement), feel free to browse that before starting these.

As before, to indicate which finger to use for each note, numbers have been included underneath the tablature. Go back and forth between the pairs of fingers while using alternate picking…

1st and 2nd finger…

1st and 3rd finger…

1st and 4th finger…

2nd and 3rd finger…

2nd and 4th finger…

3rd and 4th finger…

Although the 3rd and 4th fingers have different tendons they are connected to the same muscle in the forearm. Independence between them may need some practise.

4

If we put them all together we get the following exercise…

Here it is backwards, you might find this trickier…

The exercises are placed with the 1st finger on the 5th fret G string but you could play the "12121313 etc" finger pattern (and backwards) anywhere on the fret-board.

Minimising Movement

In the photo to the left the fingers are kept close to the fret-board. This way less movement is needed when changing between them. Try to keep the fingers near the fret-board like this when they are not in use.

To the right the fingers are not kept close to the fret-board making for unnecessary movement. This may be what comes naturally at first but it's best to aim for minimal movement until it becomes second nature.

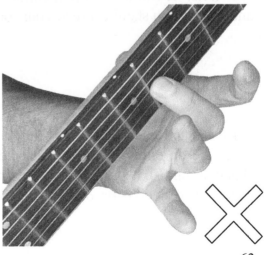

63

If you have trouble getting the correct technique (e.g. if any of your fretting fingers push against each other and aren't independent as you play), you could try moderately tensing the hand and fingers and playing very slow. This will mean all the muscles are activated *including* the ones that are actually needed but you can't yet activate on their own.

With practise the brain learns to keep the muscles that are needed active while switching off the ones that aren't. Eventually it should start to feel more natural. This technique can be effective but stop if it starts to feel a strain.

Here is a finger exercise that goes across all six strings. Use fingers 1 2 3 4 on the way up and 4 3 2 1 on the way down…

You could make up your own finger patterns using any combination of fingers 1, 2, 3 and 4. For example 1 2 4 3 on the way up the strings then 4 3 1 2 on the way down or 1 4 2 3 on the way up then 4 1 3 2 on the way down. Tough at first but variation can prepare us for whatever may be in music and don't forget you can play these exercises starting from any fret.

These exercises reflect how generally when playing you should span your fingers across four frets. It was originally mentioned on "fretting hand technique" (page 28 pictures 1 and 2) that you should spread your four fingers out across as many frets.

~

On the piano the major scale started from various root notes will look different as the notes are on either white or black keys. On the guitar we can simply move the same shape around so it starts from different root notes giving us different major scales. This process is called *Transposing by the root note* and is covered in the next section.

Transposing by the Root Note

First let's learn a new shape for the Major scale. Below to the left is the C major scale we created on page 31 and to the right is another way of playing it. As we can see it has all the same notes; **C D E F G A B C**

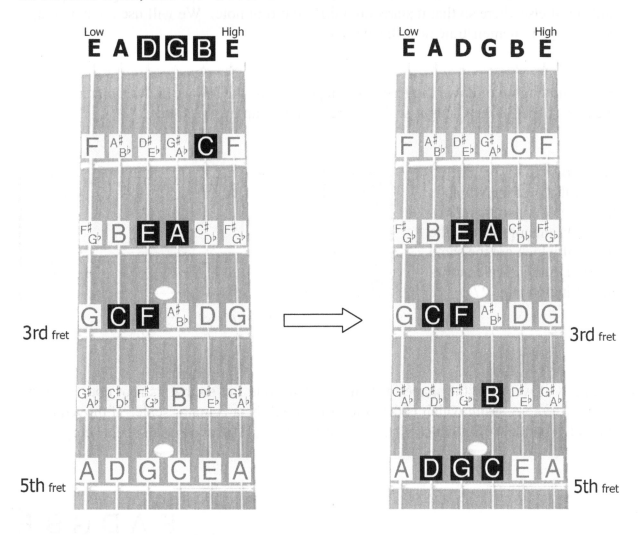

Here they are in tablature. For the new shape (on the right) you'll need to use your little finger (*4*)…

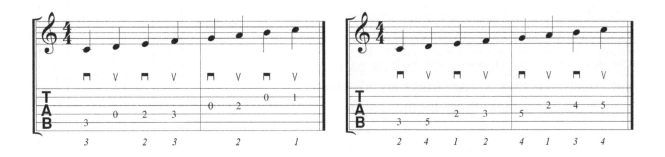

These two shapes are the most common for the major scale.

When we created the major scale across a single string on (page 24) we could start from any note for the root then apply the **TTSTTTS** formula up the string giving us different major scales (such as C major if starting on C, or F major if starting on F etc).

This principle doesn't only apply to the single string major scale; in fact it applies to anything on the fret-board. *Transposing by the root note* means taking a shape and shifting it elsewhere so that it starts on a different root note. We will use the new major scale shape to demonstrate how this works.

When moving up or down the frets, the shape remains the same. In the tablature below, the new shape for the C major scale has been moved up by two frets...

Now its root is on the 5th fret of the A string which is the note of D, so this gives us a D major scale (the notes of which are the same as the D major scale across one string on page 27).

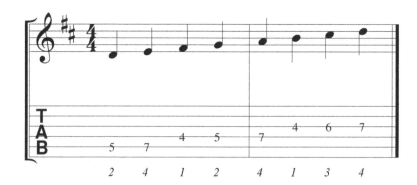

Similarly if we move the shape for C major *down* one fret so that its root note is on the 2nd fret of the A string which is the note of B, it will be a B major scale. If moved up so its root is on the 9th fret which is the note of F♯, it would be an F♯ major scale etc.

It is also mostly the case that the shape remains the same when moving it so that its root starts on different strings, however when doing so, the tuning of the B string needs to be taken into account.

To the right is the diagram we saw on page 11 for "relative tuning". The strings are all tuned equally to each other except for the B string.

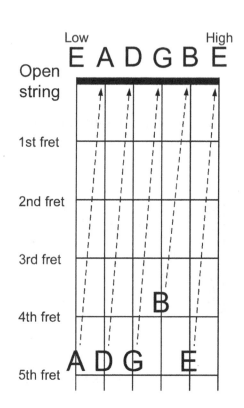

66

You've good reason to wonder why the strings can't all be tuned the same! This is because unless the B string is tuned the way it is, many chords (particularly barre chords, which are explained later) would become impossible if not much more difficult to play.

The rule is; *When part of a scale or chord shape goes over the B string, from that string upwards the shape needs to be moved up by a fret.*

If we start with the root on the low E string, or the A string (as we have already looked at) then it's fairly straightforward, the shape remains the same, the B string is not involved…

Note: The following examples have all been kept with their root on the 7th fret for convenience, and as previously mentioned the shapes remain the same if moved up or down the frets.

From low E string

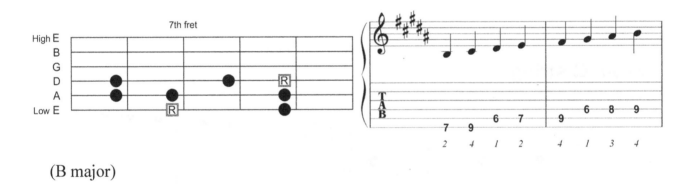

(B major)

From A string

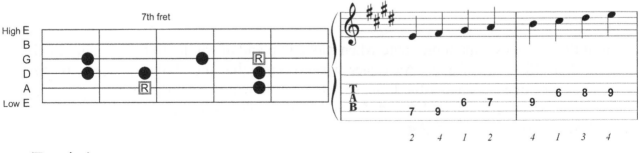

(E major)

In the following, the major scale shape has its root on the D string. The part of the scale shape that goes over the B string has been moved up by a fret...

From D string

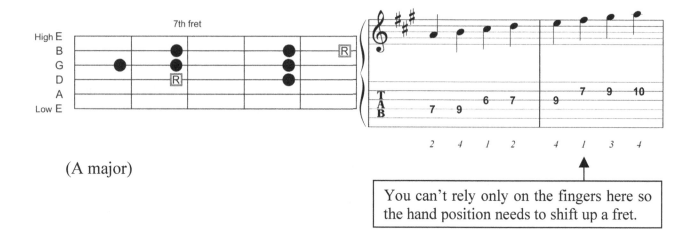

(A major)

You can't rely only on the fingers here so the hand position needs to shift up a fret.

Likewise for when its root note is on the G string the scale shape has been moved up by a fret where it goes over the B and high E string...

From G string

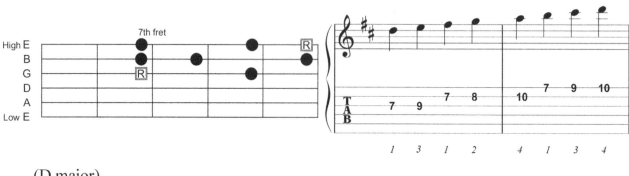

(D major)

All of these shapes remain the same when moved up and down the frets; it is only the B string that affects the shape. An easier way to remember the above shapes is by the sequence of fingers spanning the frets, so for example with the root note starting on any fret of the G string that's *1 3 1 2 4 1 3 4*. The root note starting from any fret of the low E string would be *2 4 1 2 4 1 3 4*

If we look at the chord shapes we can see how the B string affects these too. A and D major are actually from the same shape as E major but where their notes occur on the B and high E string they have been moved up by a fret...

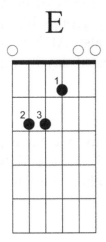

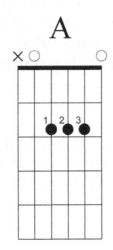

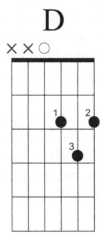

The lowest three strings of each of these chord shapes are based around the major scale shape we have just looked at.

Similarly for the minor chord shapes, A minor and D minor are from the E minor shape but moved up a fret where their notes occur past the B string...

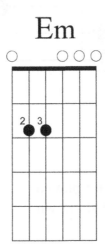

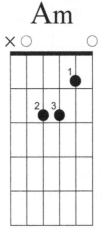

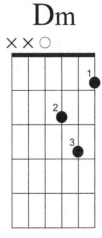

Power Chords

As the name might suggest these are often used in Rock and other forms of heavier music. Early on in the 50's power chords would have been used by groups like Bill Haley and the Comets, Status Quo in the 1970's often used them, also AC/DC with songs like "Back in Black". Of course they are also used in the present day by many Rock and Heavy metal bands.

Power chords contain only the root and perfect 5th intervals. With no 3rd there is no distinction between Major or minor. Below is the major scale shape we have just studied with its root on the low E string (it's A major). The root and 5th are highlighted to show the power chord. The higher octave of the root note has also been highlighted as it is the same note as the root...

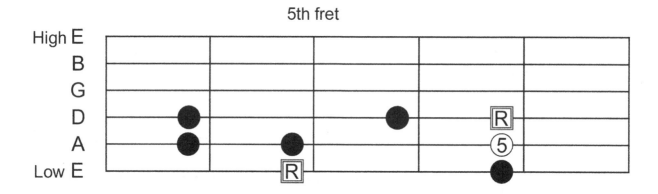

In the photo to the right these intervals are played together giving us an A power chord, also known as "A5" based on its intervals...

These chords are best fretted without using the middle finger because the stretch of two frets between the root and 5th would be a little too far for the middle and the index finger.

> **Note:** The middle finger is elevated in the photo so you can see what the other fingers are doing. Normally when fretting chords, fingers not in use should be kept closer to the fret-board.

We can also make power chords from the major scale shape with its root on the A string. To the right is a C#5 chord...

These last two power chord shapes are actually the same as the bottom three strings of A and E major open chord shapes. The intervals on those strings are also the root, 5th and octave of the root (while the interval of the 3rd is on the next string up for both E and A major). Anyway, back to power chords. Power chords are not as often played with their root on the D string. Below is a rock piece that uses power chords, written in tablature with strumming directions...

Route 5 ◎ 14 & 15

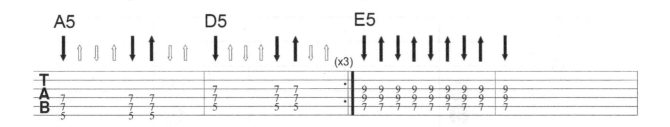

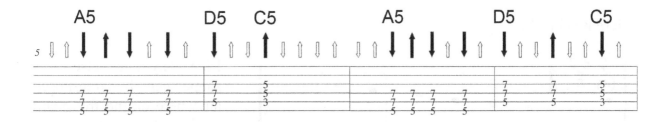

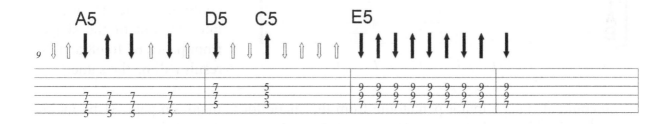

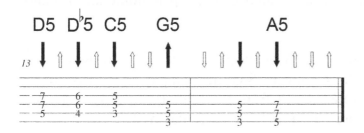

Note: For power chords, the fretting hand can be used to mute the strings that aren't played.

Pentatonic Scales

Scales that contain five notes, hence the name "penta" for five and "tonic" for notes. These scales are quite versatile with many uses. The two most common are the Major pentatonic and the Minor pentatonic, which are like the Major and Natural minor scale but with certain intervals taken out.

The Major Pentatonic

Made up of the intervals: **Root, major 2nd, major 3rd, perfect 5th and major 6th**

This is like the Major scale *without* the **perfect 4th** and **major 7th**. If we use the shape for the Major scale that we learnt in the previous section and take out these intervals then we get a "hollowed out" version. Here's the shape with its root on the low E string 5th fret, giving us an A major pentatonic scale...

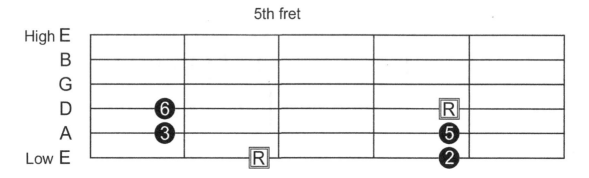

Here it is in tab...

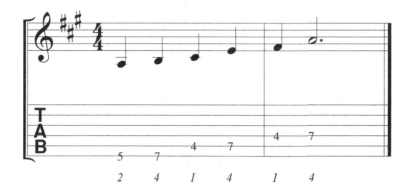

Like anything else this shape can be transposed anywhere on the fret-board (taking the B string into account). Alternatively you could take the 4th and 7th intervals out of the shapes from pages 67 to 68 and the result will be the same.

You could also get a major pentatonic from the shape for C major on page 31 by taking the 4th and 7th intervals from it. The song "My Girl" by the Temptations uses the major pentatonic scale for its repeating guitar riff; ascending C major pentatonic and F major pentatonic scales.

Over the page is a country style piece using an A major pentatonic scale. It uses 1st and 2nd endings (as we originally looked at for the piece "Summer" on page 32). Toward the end there are a few other notes added that aren't from the scale (known as *chromatic* notes) that give an interesting effect. Can you spot them when playing?

Mosey on Down

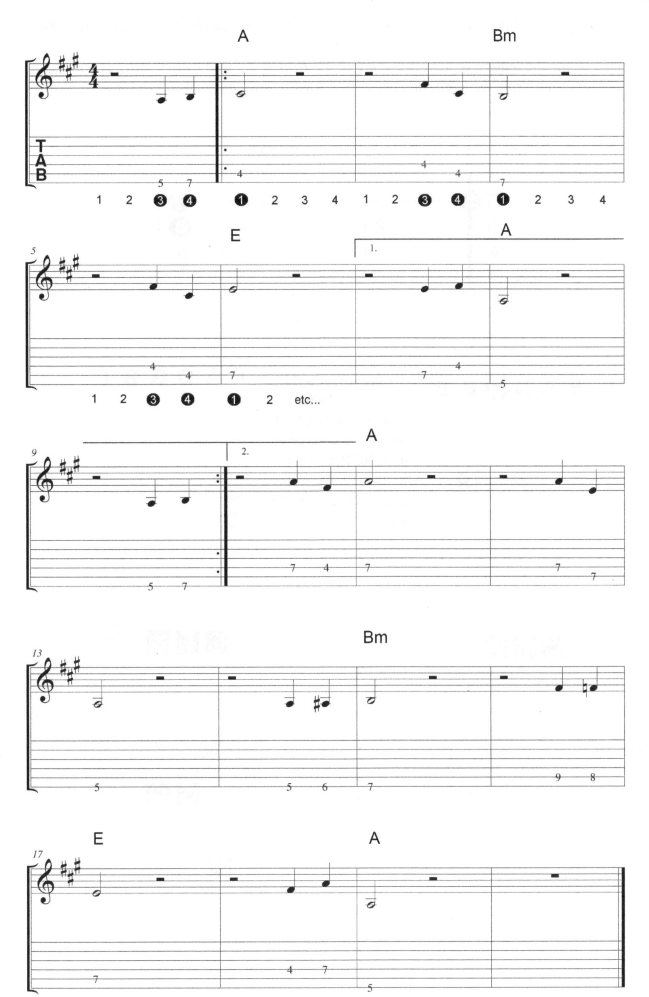

The Minor Pentatonic

Made up of the intervals: **Root, minor 3rd, perfect 4th, perfect 5th and minor 7th**

This is like the natural minor scale *without* the **major 2nd** and **minor 6th**. Below is the natural minor scale we learnt on pages 33 - 34 with those intervals taken out…

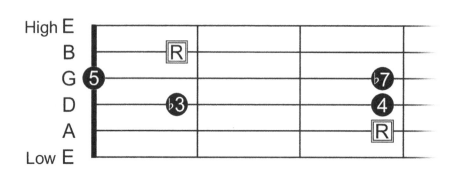

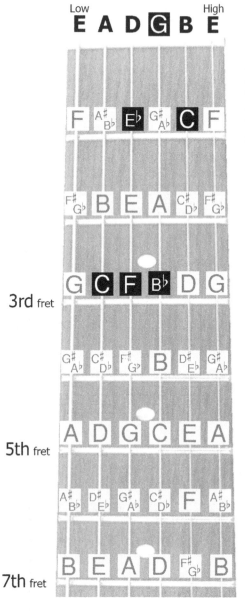

To the left it's on a fret-board diagram, and to the right it has been converted to a different shape. It has all the same notes C E♭ F G B♭…

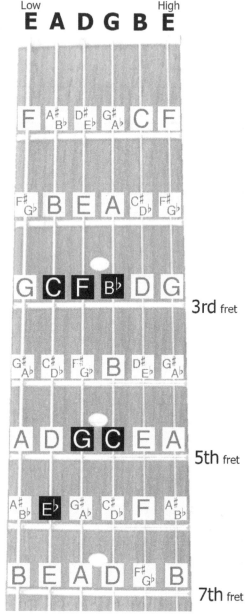

74

Let's transpose the converted shape down a string so that its root is on the low E string. The root is now on the note of G (3rd fret low E string) giving us a G minor pentatonic scale…

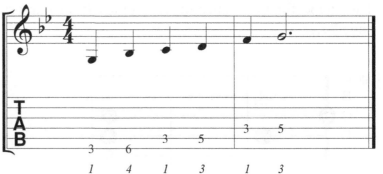

Like all the scales we have looked at so far, this one goes across one octave i.e. it starts on its root note (in this case G) and ends on the root note in a higher octave. If we also repeat the scale through a higher octave we can make use of the higher three strings as well while keeping the hand in the same area of the fret-board.

In the following diagram we can see where the two octaves of the minor pentatonic scale start and finish between the root notes…

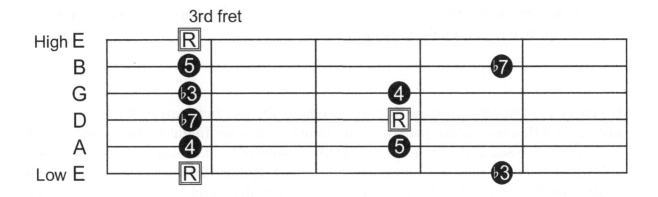

Here it is in Tab with finger numbers…

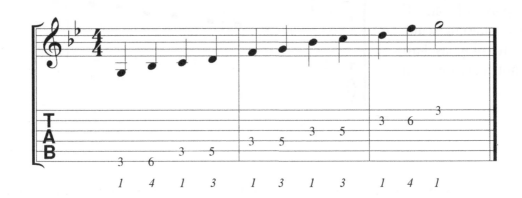

The shape for the higher octave comes from our original minor pentatonic shape on page 74…

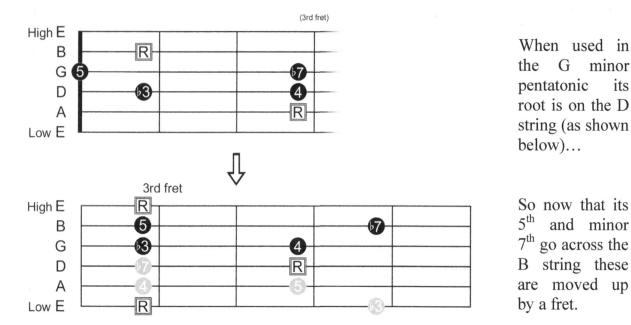

When used in the G minor pentatonic its root is on the D string (as shown below)…

So now that its 5th and minor 7th go across the B string these are moved up by a fret.

In relation to the root the higher octave of the root note hasn't shifted up a fret because it was already on the B string for the original shape, so it still shares the same fret as the minor 3rd (which is now on the G string).

If you've got this far well done that was probably the toughest part of the book, so it's just as well this two-octave pattern of the minor pentatonic might be the most popular and frequently used scale on the guitar. Many famous riffs and solos are based around it and variations of it, such as by Eric Clapton, Pink Floyd and BB King. It's also behind many bass lines too, such as "Hit Me with your Rhythm Stick" by Ian Drury and the Blockheads and "Play that Funky Music" by Wild Cherry.

Basic blues (page 19) used part of an E minor pentatonic scale. Easier to play as half of its notes are on open strings…

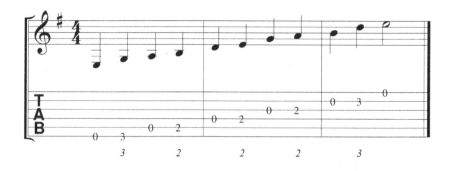

On the next page is a Rock melody based on the G minor pentatonic scale we have just covered…

Headstrong 18&19

This piece uses **D.C.** but also a Coda $\oplus$. *"al Coda"* (just after D.C.) means *apply the coda*. The coda acts like a teleport. Play to the end of the second line then go back to the beginning but this time when you get to the coda at the end of bar 4, go straight to where you see the other coda (9th bar) and play from there to the end.

Chapter 4 Questions

1. *How many shapes are the most common for the major scale? two or three?*

2. *When moving a shape up or down the frets does the shape change?*

3. *When moving a shape up or down the frets does the root note and therefore scale change?*

4. *If moving a shape to different strings what string needs to be considered if the scale goes over it?*

5. *What happens when a scale goes over that string?*

6. *What are the intervals of a power chord?*

7. *What number comes after the root note to represent a power chord?*

8. *How many notes in a pentatonic scale?*

9. *What are the intervals of a Major pentatonic scale?*

10. *What are the intervals of a minor pentatonic scale?*

11. *How many octaves does the most popular pattern for the minor pentatonic repeat through?*

(You will find the answers at the back of the book)

Sight-reading

So far, for the previous musical exercises, numbers have been placed below to help with the rhythm because tablature on its own gives little indication about this. Often when someone wants to learn a song, they use the tablature, and although being familiar with the piece and having a "feel" for it is good, unless we are perfect at that, rhythm reading can help ensure we are playing all of it right. So to get a full idea of a piece the guitarist should at least learn some rhythm reading from the staff.

How long in time a note lasts, is the *note value,* which is indicated by what symbol is used for the note. The following three are commonly used note values…

Whole note   Half note   Quarter note

Here are these note values relative to each other…

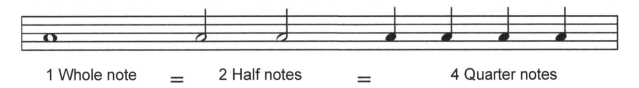

1 Whole note   **=**   2 Half notes   **=**   4 Quarter notes

When you tap your foot or count over a piece of music these are the *beats*. To tell us how to count a piece of music a *Time signature* is used. This appears on the Staff at the start of a piece, just to the right of the clef as two numbers, one on top of the other. The example below shows the Staff as it normally would be above the tab…

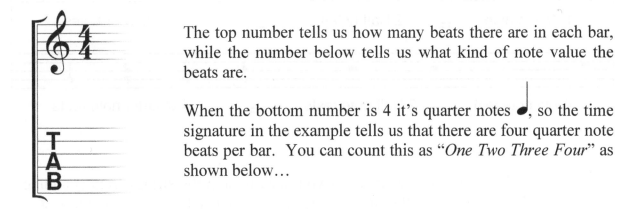

The top number tells us how many beats there are in each bar, while the number below tells us what kind of note value the beats are.

When the bottom number is 4 it's quarter notes ♩, so the time signature in the example tells us that there are four quarter note beats per bar. You can count this as "*One Two Three Four*" as shown below…

1 2 3 4   1 2 3 4   1 2 3 4   1 2 3 4

You don't have to *play* four quarter notes per bar. There can be any kind of actual notes as long as they add up to fit the duration of the bar, such as in the example below.

Two half notes in the first bar followed by two quarter notes and a half note in the next bar…

Here are a couple of rhythms for you to try. They are in 4 / 4 time and use the three note values we've just covered. Numbers have been added underneath to help with counting. Clap (or play open G string) where the notes occur…

1.

2.

A *Rest* is a pause in music, indicating when *not* to play. Every note value has an equivalent rest. Here are the note values relative to each other again, but with their corresponding rests included underneath…

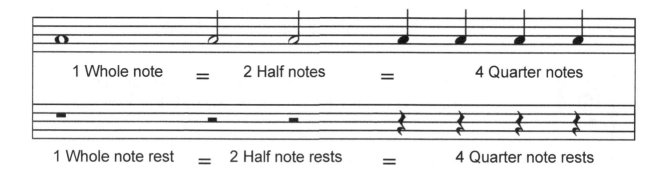

| 1 Whole note | = | 2 Half notes | = | 4 Quarter notes |

| 1 Whole note rest | = | 2 Half note rests | = | 4 Quarter note rests |

When there is a rest you need to stop the strings from sounding, this is called *string damping*. Use the side of your hand to rest on the strings until the next note occurs. Alternatively you could use the fretting hand by gently releasing the pressure from the fretting finger.

Here are a couple of rhythms. Again they are in 4 / 4 time and use the three note values, but now some are rests. It would be best to play them on the guitar rather than clap so that you can account for the rests…

1.

2.

Let's look at another two kinds of smaller note values. The Eighth note and Sixteenth note…

Here are these note values relative to a quarter note and to each other with their corresponding rests included underneath. When note values smaller than a quarter note occur next to each other their stems are often barred together.

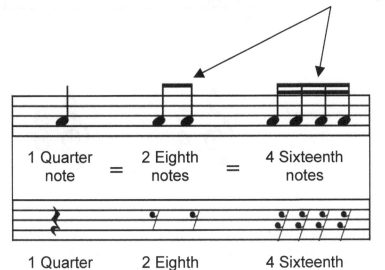

Rests are never joined together.

There are some rhythms that contain these note values on the next section "How to Keep Time". For now let's look at some more time signatures.

So far we have only looked at 4 / 4 time, the most common time signature, sometimes indicated with a large "C" for "Common Time". Below are some examples of other types of time signature.

Three quarter note beats per bar…

When the bottom number is 2 this refers to half notes ♩ therefore this time signature is two half note beats per bar…

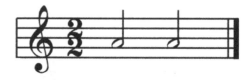

When the bottom number is 8 this refers to eighth notes ♪ therefore this time signature is six eighth note beats per bar...

What do you think these time signatures mean?

An example of 9/8 time would be the Carpet-baggers theme tune from Jimmy Smith's Album "The Cat". If you listen to it you might be able to tell its timing is odd. These last two time signatures are known as *odd time*.

How to Keep Time (When reading rhythm from the staff)

To read music rhythm accurately, you need to take into account where in time all the notes are within each bar. To do this we need to count. How to count will depend on what the smallest note value is.

The following explanations show how this is done. The strongest beat(s) are written in **bold** as it helps to emphasise them while counting. Following each explanation is a rhythmical exercise to clap or play while counting.

If any piece is in 4 / 4 time and has no smaller note value than quarter notes, counting "**One** Two Three Four" or "**One** Two **Three** Four" is appropriate…

If any piece is in 4 / 4 time and has no smaller note value than eighth notes, counting "**One** and Two and Three and Four and" or "**One** and Two and **Three** and Four and" enables us to account for the eighth notes too…

For 3 / 4 time, when quarter notes are the smallest note value you would count "**One** Two Three"…

In 3 / 4 time, if eighth notes are the smallest note value, counting "**One** and Two and Three and" enables us to account for the eighth notes too…

If any piece is in 6 / 8 and there is no smaller note value than eighth notes we can count "**One** Two Three **Four** Five Six"…

If in a 4 / 4 piece of music sixteenth notes are the smallest note value we can count "**One** e and a Two e and a Three e and a Four e and a" or "**One** e and a Two e and a **Three** e and a Four e and a" to take the sixteenth notes into account also…

There are other time signatures but these are the most often used. The same principle always applies; count according to the smallest note value and emphasise the strongest beat(s).

Now that we've learnt a few things about reading rhythm from conventional notation let's put it into practise and use it in conjunction with tablature. The following pieces (starting on the next page) range from simple to the more difficult. Some you are probably familiar with, which might help if you can tell if it sounds wrong, others you won't be familiar with so will need to rely more on reading them.

Twinkle Twinkle Little Star

As previously mentioned for "Basic blues" (page 18) it can help to focus on the melody and rhythm separately at first.

Frere Jacques

Piece 1 - Merry Dance

This piece you won't be familiar with. Don't forget its time signature is different from the last two pieces.

Dotted Notes - A dot just after a note increases its value by half.

Half of a half note is a quarter note, so a dotted half note lasts a quarter note longer (or three quarter notes altogether).

Here are some rhythm exercises. They happen to be on the note of B which means the stem of the note goes down to keep it neat (as was explained on the bottom of page 15)...

1.

2.

Half of a quarter note is an eighth note, so a dotted quarter note lasts an eighth note longer (or three eighth notes altogether).

Here are some rhythm exercises...

1.

2.

Greensleeves

For this piece, make sure you play the first note on the third beat of the first bar. Like the last piece on page 86 (Merry Dance) this one is also in 𝄞 3/4 time.

Piece 2 - Pirates Jig

Now back to using 6/4 time. This unfamiliar piece uses dotted half and quarter notes.

Tied Notes

A tie is a curved line connecting two notes of the same pitch. When two notes are tied the first note is extended by the value of the note that it is tied to, so the first note lasts longer. Below are a few examples.

Here a half note is tied to an eighth note, making it last an eighth note longer. You could also see this as lasting for two quarter notes and an eighth note (or five eighth notes)....

Here an eighth note is tied to a quarter note making it last a quarter note longer. You could also see this as lasting for three eighth notes...

Here a quarter note is tied to a half note. You could also see this as lasting for three quarter notes...

Here are rhythm exercises that have some tied notes. Remember the tied note is held *not* played as though it's a new note...

1.

2.

Ties can be useful for when a note lasts longer than the bar that it is in. In the following piece dotted half notes are extended over the bar by another half note to make each last for five (quarter note) beats altogether...

Amazing Grace

Similar to Greensleeves on page 88 for this piece the first note comes in on the third beat of the first bar.

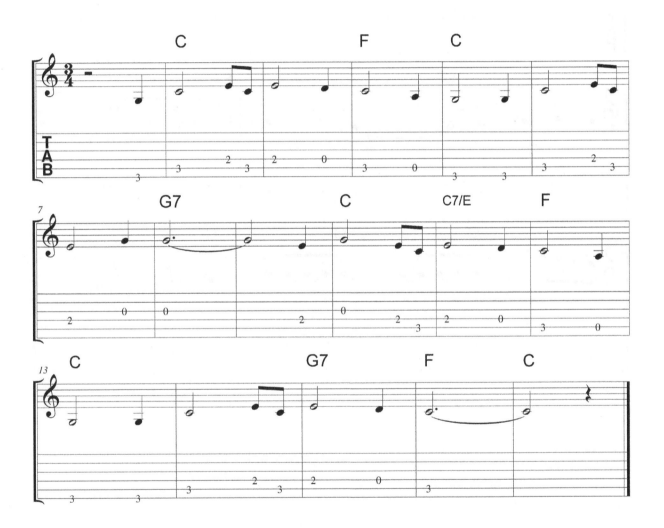

Piece 3 - Memories

This unfamiliar piece has tied whole notes, tied half notes and tied eighth notes.

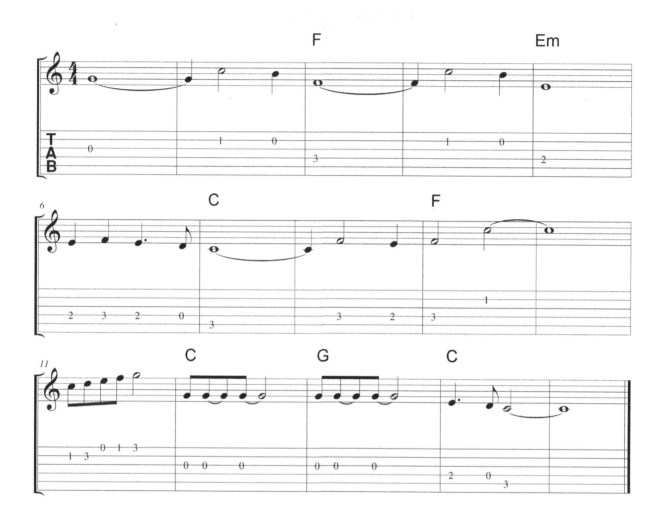

Here are some more short pieces that you won't be familiar with. The first is simple.

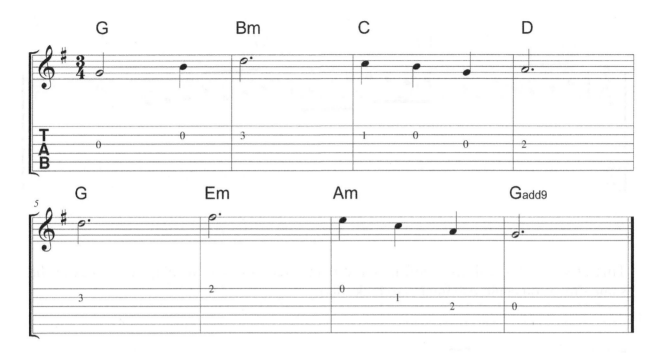

The notes in this piece are all from a G major scale (its shape with the root note on the open G string like on page 68)…

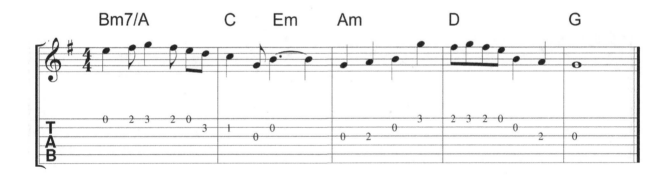

From the same shape but now Major pentatonic…

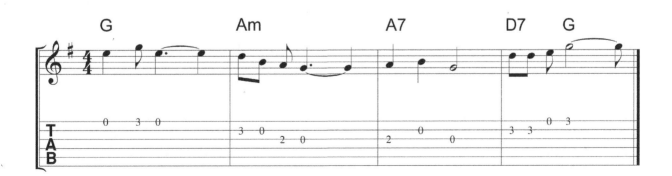

This is a Motown style riff using A minor pentatonic…

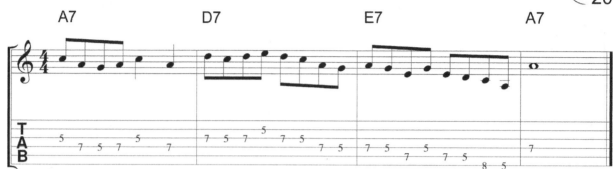

This piece is classical style and in some places requires you to play two notes at the same time (you could use fingers to pick this)…

Sight Strumming

Seeing as we have just studied the rhythmical aspect of sight-reading, it makes sense to continue with rhythm guitar. For rhythm reading on its own, the notation can be adapted to hash marks that match the original note symbols…

Quarter note   Eighth note

…or when more than one in a row…

The exercises in this section are all in 4 / 4 time and the smallest note value is an eighth note. First of all let's start with a bar full of eighth notes. This is similar to underlying movement near the bottom of page 53.

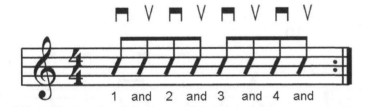

Arches and downward points have been added to show the strumming directions.   Arches for down and points for up.

Choose any chord you know then strum it to these rhythms. Compared to the first section on strumming (page 50 - 60) the difference with these is that the ghost strums are not indicated, only the actual strums are, so you need to work out the motion for the strumming hand between the strums. For the first two exercises numbers have been added underneath to show when the chords are strummed…

1.   2.

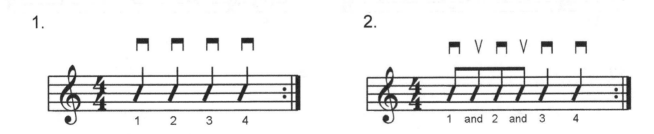

Only play on the quarter notes, with upward ghost strums in-between.

There's an upward ghost strum between beats 3 and 4 making them as far apart in time as beats 1 and 2.

3.

4.

5.

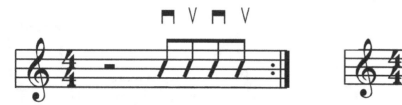

6.

7.

8.

9.

10.

11.

12.

13.

14.

15.

16.

These strumming patterns can be also used in conjunction with the exercises from the tutorial "Changing between Chords" (pages 43 - 49). You could choose one of the patterns and use it over all four bars of an exercise from that tutorial. Best to start with the simpler chord sequences and strumming patterns (or at whatever level you are at) then work your way up.

For the following pieces read from the chord names on top and strum a rhythm. For Bayou Noir strumming pattern 1 would be the easiest. When you feel more confident try other patterns such as 3, 7 or 8 which sound appropriate to the Cajun style, although you could use any of the patterns you like…

Bayou Noir 21&22

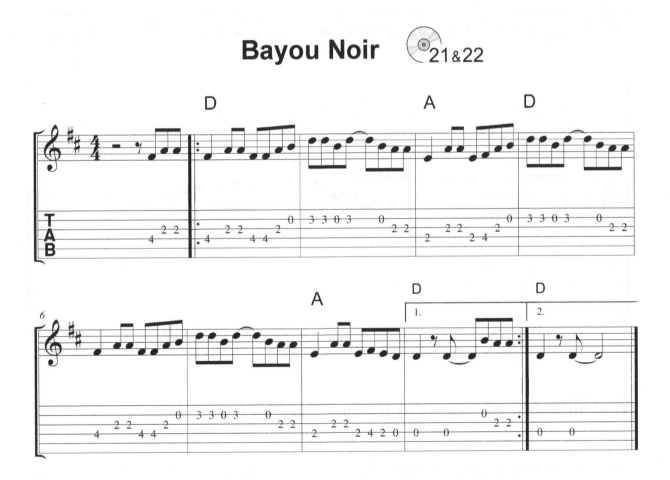

For Florida Blues (over the page) most bars have two chords in, so the changes need to be quicker.

This piece is in swing feel. For swing feel, the second eighth note of every pair of eighth notes comes in slightly later as if the rhythm is skipping from one note to another. To the right

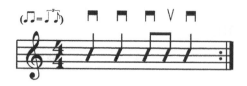

is a suggested strumming pattern with a pair of eighth notes on the third beat (this is on the demo track). In the last bar of the second line there are three chords. Use pattern 1 (page 95) for this bar as it's easier and works better musically…

Florida Blues   23&24

Working out Strumming Patterns by Ear

If you want to work out a strumming pattern from hearing it, first listen to the piece and work out it's beat by counting to it. This is usually no more complicated than how you would tap your foot to a piece of music. Once you have done this, ghost strum to it and try to be aware of where the strums are as you do. When you think you've worked out where the actual strums are play them as you move your arm.

98

Chapter 5 Questions

1. *What does the "note value" mean?*

2. *How many quarter notes in a whole note?*

3. *How many quarter notes in a half note?*

4. *What does the top number in a time signature tell us?*

5. *What does the bottom number in a time signature tell us?*

6. *What does this time signature mean?*

7. *What kind of note value is this?*

8. *How many of them in a quarter note?*

9. *What kind of rest is this?*

10. *When note values less than a quarter note occur next to each other what often happens to their stems?*

11. *When counting to a piece of music it helps to emphasise what beats?*

12. *How much does a dot just after a note extend the note by?*

13. *If a note lasts longer than the bar that it is in, what can be used to solve this?*

14. *What is the value of this note i.e. how long would it last?* **O.**

15. *When two notes are tied together how many notes do you actually play?*

Movable Barre Chords

A barre is when a finger presses down across multiple strings on the same fret. On the picture below left the 1st finger is barring across the 6th fret.

As shown below, if we place the shape of the E major open chord in front of the barre, then we have transposed the entire chord upward including the notes that were on the open strings. The 2nd, 3rd, and 4th fingers are used for the chord shape as the 1st finger is needed for the barre...

To make the barre easier at first, you could rotate the index finger a little towards its outer side and place its joints roughly where the strings need to be pushed down on the frets. Also, placing the thumb more behind the index finger rather than its usual place (of roughly behind the middle finger) can make it easier to apply pressure on the barre.

The fret-board diagram below shows the notes of the low E string so that we can find the root note of the barre chord and therefore what the chord is. The 6th fret is the note of A$^{\sharp}$ (or B$^{\flat}$) so that is the root note of the above chord, therefore it is an A$^{\sharp}$ (or B$^{\flat}$) major chord.

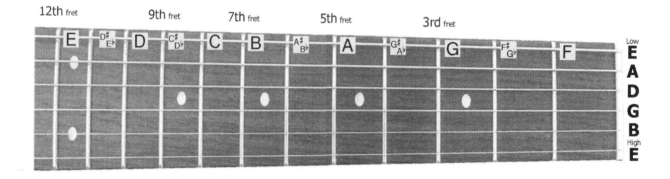

We can shift this barre chord shape up and down the fret-board to get different chords. Over the page are some more examples...

Here's G major...

We can make minor chords by putting the shape from E minor open chord (page 41) in front of the barre. To the right is A minor...

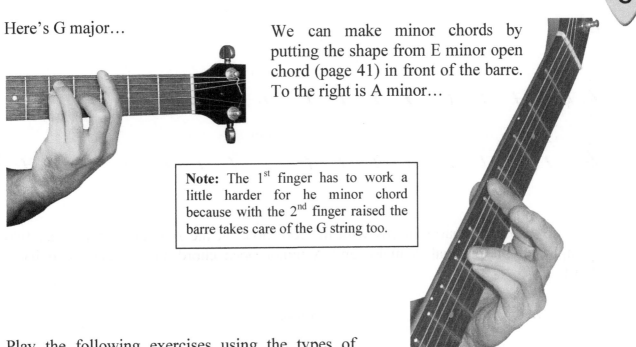

> **Note:** The 1ˢᵗ finger has to work a little harder for he minor chord because with the 2ⁿᵈ finger raised the barre takes care of the G string too.

Play the following exercises using the types of barre chord just covered. You can use the diagram on the previous page to find the roots...

Ex. 1

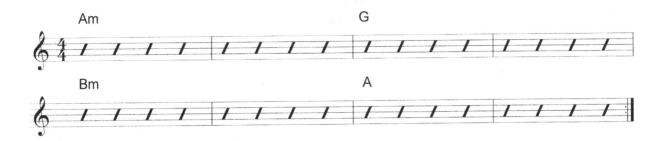

The next exercise (over the page) uses F major barre chord. Barre chords lower down the neck need a bit more pressure as you are pushing down near to where the strings are held up by the nut.

F

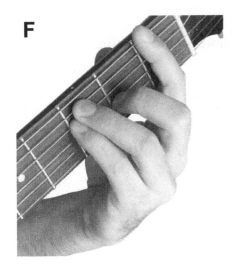

To the right is an easier version where you don't play the low E and A strings. The 3ʳᵈ fret of the D string is the note of F so the lowest note is still the root note...

F (EZ)

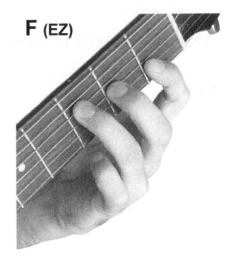

Ex. 2

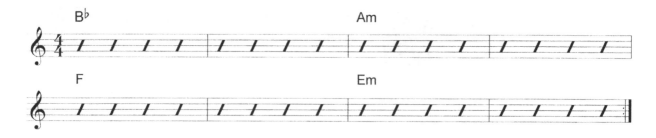

You can also make barre chords with the root note on the A string. Below are two examples of the original A major and A minor open chord shapes made into barre chords.

B major...   D# minor...

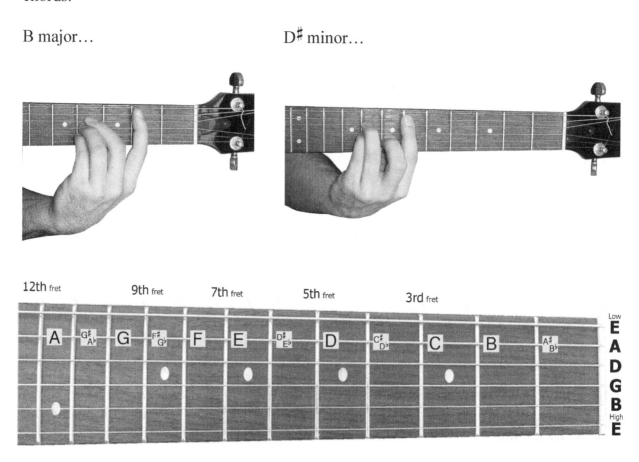

Play the chords in the following exercises with their root note on the A string...

Ex. 1

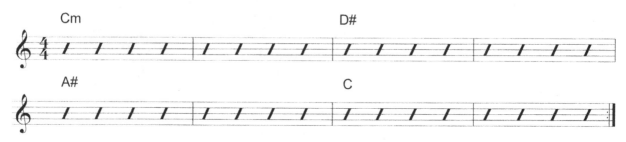

Ex. 2

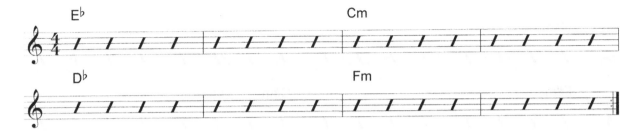

If we play the chords with their root notes on both the low E and A string there is less movement up and down the neck. In the following exercises the barre chords could be either with their root on the low E or the A string, whichever means less movement to get to the next chord. Feel free to write next to each chord (in pencil) the string and fret that the root note is on if this helps…

Ex. 1

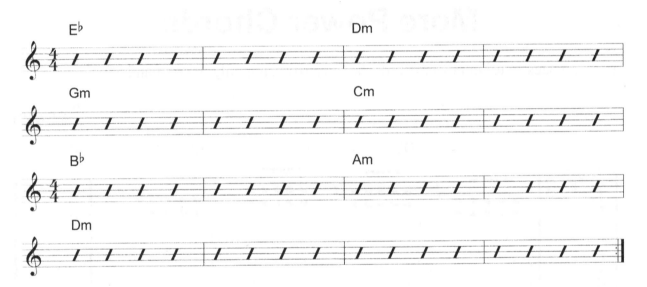

Ex. 2

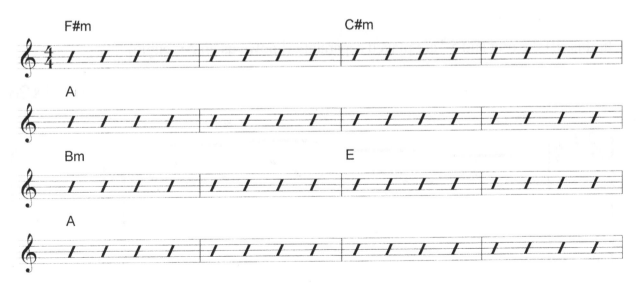

Ex. 3

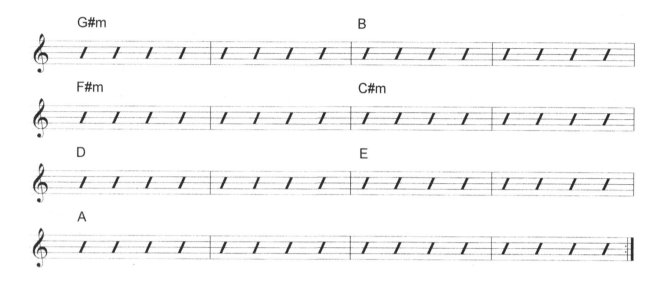

More Power Chords

Let's go back to using power chords, here's a riff using only the root and 5th...

25 & 26

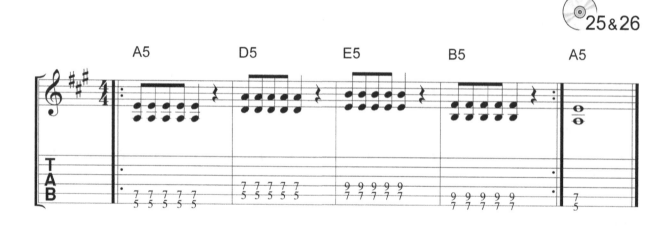

In this riff the root and 5th are played separately (known as an Arpeggio).

27 & 28

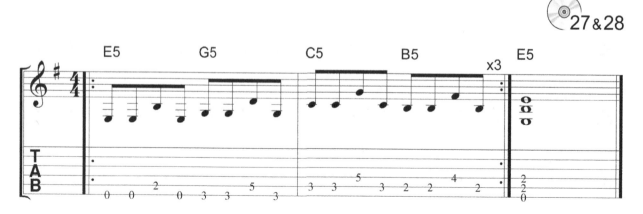

In this piece the chords are played with the octave of the root also.

The Bikers Entered the Room

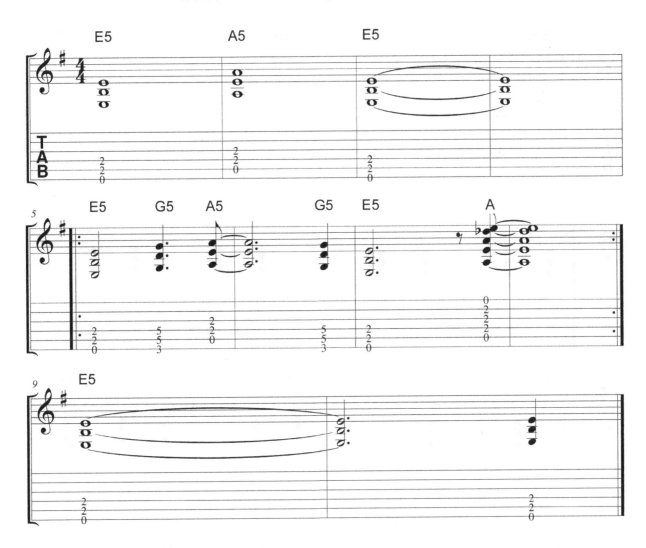

In some styles of heavier music lower tuning and fast changes between power chords are required, so "drop D" is often used. This is done by tuning the low E string down to the note of D.

This way, when playing a power chord with its root on the low E string (now D) all of its notes will be on the same fret because the root needs to be moved two frets higher to compensate for the lower tuning. This makes power chords easier to play and move up and down the fret-board with because we can barre across with one finger.

In the photo is a G5 chord played in drop D tuning, barred with the 3rd finger. In this example it's being reinforced with the 2nd finger, although ideally you want to be able to barre with a finger on its own.

Here is a heavy metal style piece that uses drop D power chords containing the root, 5th and octave…

Heavy D

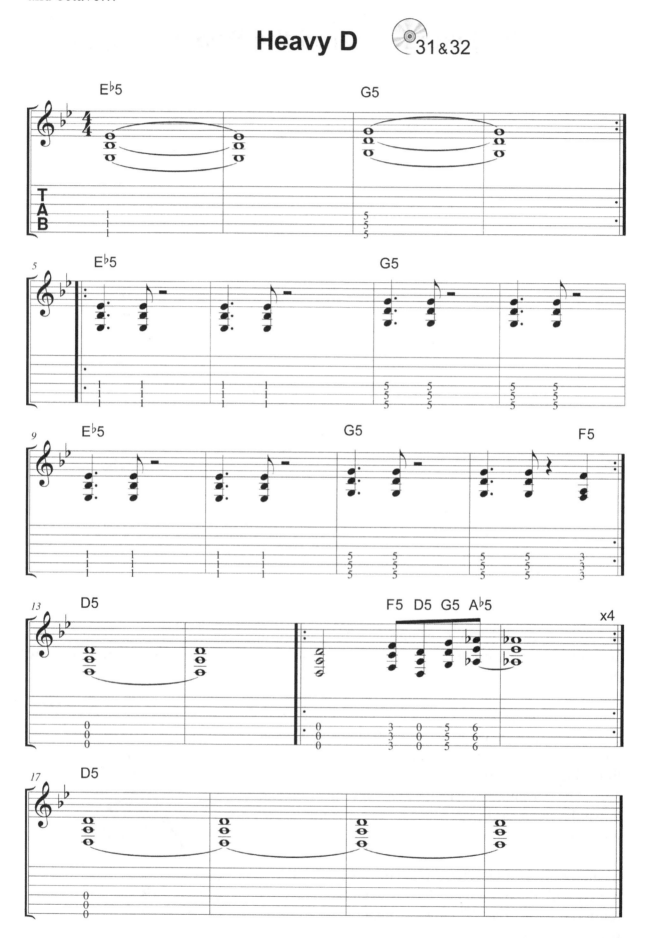

Palm Muting

Palm muting makes the guitar sound more rhythmically defined. The notes become shorter, giving them a tight chunky quality. It can be used in many styles but particularly Funk, Rock or Blues.

Rest the side of your palm lightly across the strings just off the bridge as you play. The first photo shows where the side of the palm should be. In the second photo the side of the palm is resting lightly on the strings just off the bridge as the hand plays.

1.

2.

The further away from the bridge and onto the strings you rest the palm the more muting there is, so try not to go too far and completely mute the strings! Also if you have a movable bridge, try not to move it while you are playing.

Palm muting is indicated with "P.M." above the music with a dotted line for as long as you are supposed to use it.

P.M. — — — — |

The following pieces are in swing feel (we first looked at this for Florida Blues on page 98). First is a bluesy riff using palm muting, play with downward strokes only across the two strings to get the desired pumping rhythmical effect...

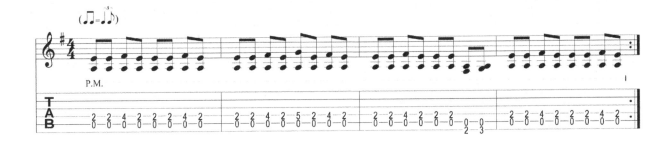

a couple more over the page...

Travelling Man

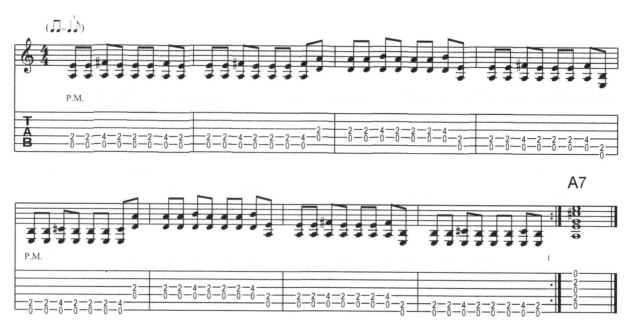

Here's a trickier one…

Boogie Boy

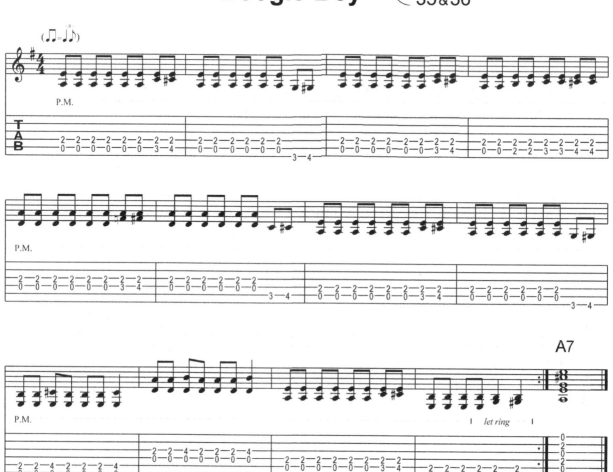

108

Lead Playing Techniques

There are many techniques you can use for lead playing. Here are some basic and often used ones.

Hammer-ons and Pull-offs - A hammer-on is placing a fretting finger down on a fret to play a note without plucking the string, as though you are "hammering" on with the finger.

Play the 5th fret of the G string with the index finger.

While this note is ringing use the 3rd finger to hammer onto the 7th fret of the same string.

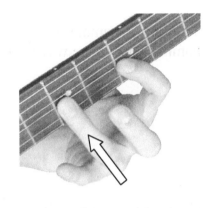

You can use any fingers, string and frets you like (as long as you can reach). Try and place the finger that is hammering on as accurately as you can. Practise this at a slow speed at first.

A hammer-on is indicated with a curved line going from one note to another higher note. To the right is an example of how a hammer-on would be written…

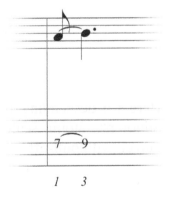

A pull-off is the opposite of a hammer-on. Pull the finger off the fret where it has just played and as you do, move it down slightly so it plucks the string as it leaves. This will play the note behind (be that an open string or a fretted note). Try not to hit other strings with the finger as it pulls off, and avoid leaving the finger on the string for too long before it pulls off otherwise you might end up bending the string.

109

A pull-off is indicated with a curved line going from one note to another lower note…

To practise hammer-ons and pull-offs you could play the minor pentatonic scale using hammer-ons on the way up and pull-offs on the way down.

Here's an ascending B minor pentatonic scale played with hammer-ons…

Here's a descending E minor pentatonic scale played with pull-offs…

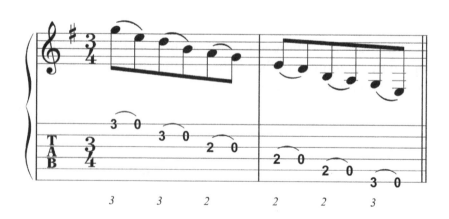

110

String Bends

Note: If you're using an Acoustic it's OK to skip to the next technique.

This is bending a string in order to bend the pitch of the note. In the photo to the left the 3rd finger is bending the G string in a downward direction, while in the photo to the right the 3rd finger is bending the B string in an upward direction…

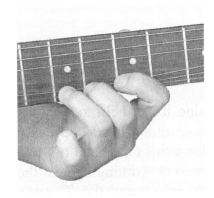

Whether you bend the string in an upward or downward direction the note will always become higher in pitch.

In both instances we can see that the other fingers behind the 3rd finger are reinforcing the string bend. This is a common technique because often the 3rd finger might not have enough strength on its own to bend the string to the desired pitch.

Bends are indicated with an arrow rising from a note with a quantity on top. The quantity indicates how far in pitch the bend needs to go, "full" is for a tone "1/2" is for a semitone. We will start with the easiest, the partial bend indicated with "1/4" often used in Blues music. Try the bends from the following exercises on their own, then again but with the note that comes after.

Use the 3rd finger to bend the G string upward slightly by less than a semitone, the following note is played with the 1st finger…

Use the 3rd finger to bend the high E string up by a semitone. For the note that follows use the 1st finger…

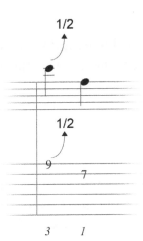

Use the 3rd finger to bend the B string upward by a tone…

To know how far to bend you need to listen. When practising it can help to play the desired note on its higher fret before bending. So before a semitone bend you could play one fret higher to hear how far you need to bend, and for a full tone bend it's two frets higher. String bends are easier on higher frets as you are not working against the nut holding the strings in place (hence why these exercises are around the 7th fret). Thinner gauge strings also help, which is why bends are more often used on electric guitars.

Sliding
- Also known as Glissando. Sliding a finger up or down the frets on the same string. For this your hand can't stay in a fixed position, it needs to move up or down the neck. So the trick is to stop the slide at the intended fret.

An upward slide is indicated with an upward line between two notes. Use the index finger for the example…

A downward slide is indicated with a downward line between two notes. Use the 3rd finger for the example…

Now that we've covered these techniques let's put it all together to give us a Bluesy solo on the next page. If you're using an acoustic guitar, for the two bends on the last line you could use slides instead (up by a semitone then a tone)…

B Minor Blues

 37 & 38

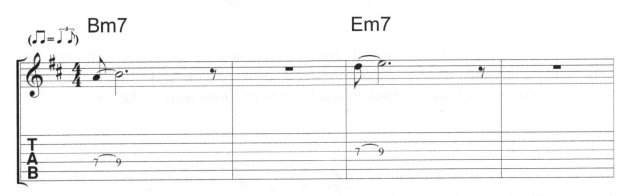

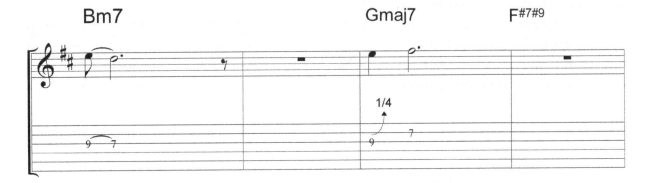

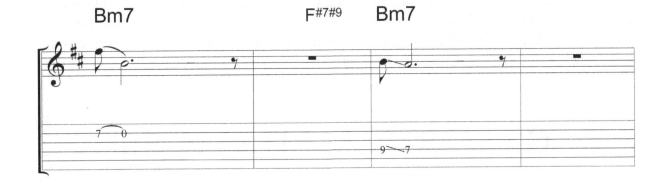

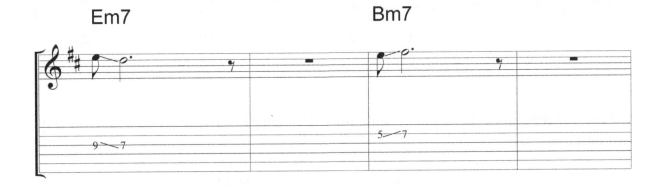

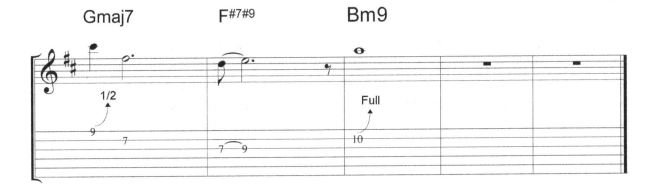

Improvising

Despite its name, improvising is usually based around at least one scale. Following are some backing tracks with scale suggestions and ideas. At the end of this section are some tips. You can also use the backing tracks from previous parts of the book.

Here's a G major scale we can use to improvise over the following chord progression. If you remember back to "Transposing by the root note" this is the major scale starting with its root on the G string from page 68.

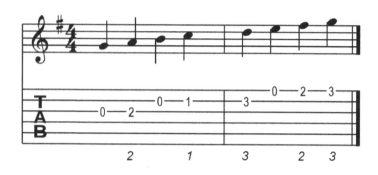

Numbers have been added underneath to help indicate the beats. Although the G major scale will fit with the chord sequence some notes may sound better than others, depending on where the note is and on what chord. You can experiment and use your ears to find what you like the sound of. To start off you could also use the suggestions written below...

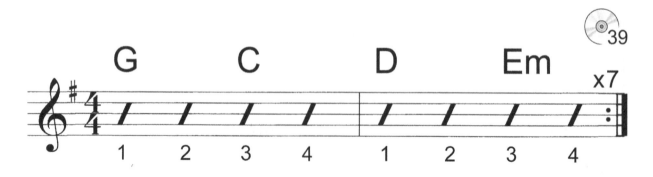

1. Play one note from the G major scale over each chord. So that's one note for every two beats.

2. Play a different note for every beat, so now you are playing twice as fast at one note per beat.

3. Play a different note on beats one, two and three of each bar (the note on the third beat can last over the fourth beat too). Now we have phrases consisting of three notes. The third note is important as it occurs on the chord change, the two notes that come before lead up to it. See what phrases you can create when doing this.

Here's another progression you can use with G major…

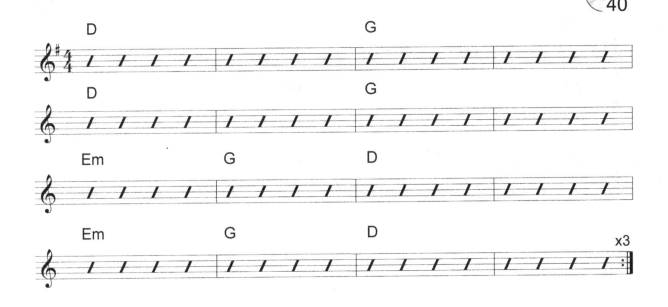

and another…

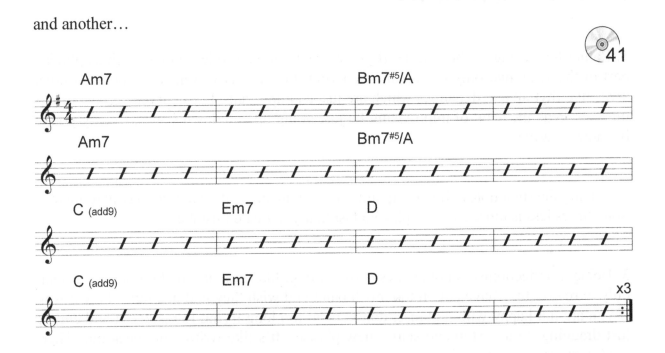

As previously mentioned some notes may sound better than others, it depends on where the note is and on what chord. You can experiment and use your ears to find what you like the sound of.

For the following 12 bar Blues chord sequence use E minor pentatonic...

42

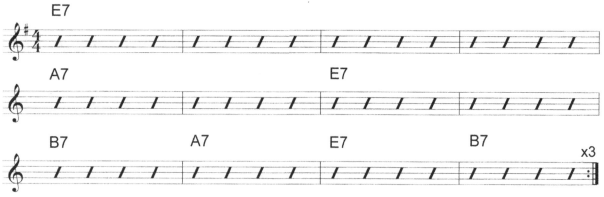

Hints for Improvising

1. Rather than using a whole scale, if you restrict yourself to less notes, such as playing part of the scale that only occurs on one string, this means you have to focus on other areas like rhythm and dynamics which are just as important. If you avoid certain strings this can break the habit of improvising by just going up and down scales, forcing you to be more creative.

2. Playing the right notes. It is the quality not the quantity of what you play that matters. Sometimes less is more so don't play so fast that you make mistakes.

3. Being a perfectionist is not always a good thing, like a painter making improvements only to realize they have put on too much paint and wish they had just left it how it was. If you are not happy with a phrase, don't spend too long trying to resolve it and end up just dragging it out. Stop and start a new phrase. It's like writing or speaking. There are full stops, commas and pauses etc.

4. Don't wander aimlessly around the fret-board. Tell a story, have a plot with a start and finish.

Chapter 6 Questions

1. *What is a barre?*

2. *For barre chords based on the original A major or A minor open chord shapes, what string is the root note on?*

3. *For barre chords based on the original E major and E minor open chord shapes, what string is the root note on?*

4. *What is the term used to describe when the low E string is tuned down to the note of D?*

5. *How can power chords be played when the low E string is tuned down to the note of D?*

6. *What does P.M. mean?*

7. *What does it mean when a curved line joins one note to another higher note?*

8. *What does it mean when a curved line joins one note to another lower note?*

9. *What if the line joining the two notes is straight?*

10. *What does this mean above a note?*   1/2

(You will find the answers at the back of the book)

How to Practise

How much practise? - 30 minutes practise 5 or 6 days a week is better than 2 to 3 hours in one day of the week. If you start to feel that it's a strain physically or mentally and your playing becomes dull, then perhaps it is best to stop and come back later. Full concentration can only last so long, so don't be fooled into ending up confused at how you got something right the first time yet after a while your playing seems to be getting worse. Perhaps it's just that your hand is tired or your concentration is becoming exhausted. Only when something becomes second nature can you continue for longer. Try not to play constantly for more than 10 minutes without a small 1 - 2 minute break and always pay attention to your fingers. If it hurts then stop! if your fingers feel like they are *about* to start "complaining" then have a break for a couple of minutes.

Patience can be fast - Being patient and having time for what might be called "serious boring stuff" is faster than being impatient, doing just the "fun" stuff and you're playing not progressing. Rather than just playing around on the guitar with your favourite tunes for 30 minutes, try to spend the first 10 minutes doing technical exercises and / or scales to a metronome. This way you'll progress faster than if you just played the guitar for 30 minutes. Then the fun stuff becomes more fun because you are better at it rather than reaching a frustrating point where you feel you can't go any further.

Playing Music - A mistake that can be made is to try and play a piece how you want it to sound as opposed to playing it how you are actually able to play it. If you can't play a whole piece well and consistently, you could isolate the more difficult parts and practise them to a metronome at a slower speed at which you can play accurately. As you get better bring it back up to speed until it fits in the song and you can play the whole thing consistently. You can make more improvement in less time this way. The same applies to playing over a backing track, practise without it first.

Likewise for scales, parts of a scale can be harder than other parts. Some might play the hard parts slower and the easier parts faster. For example with the minor pentatonic scale (one of the most used scales on the guitar), the notes on the lower strings might be harder to stretch to so a beginner might be play them slower than the rest of the scale. If you learn and practise technical exercises / scales to a metronome you develop a sense of tempo and it trains you to play consistently, so play the entire scale at a speed you can play the most difficult part adequately. Playing at a speed too fast for your ability can actually be practising making mistakes and make you worse!

Sense of timing is a skill in its own right - Sometimes less experienced players may tend to play too fast over a slower tempo i.e. a slower piece or a metronome set to a slow speed. Although this may seem contrary to earlier advice, it is often because they are playing to their technical ability rather than concentrating on actually playing in time. Technical ability on it's own means little without a sense of timing. Having your own internal metronome can help keep rhythm, such as tapping your foot to a piece of music.

General

1. Always try to give yourself a slight challenge. Not too easy but not too hard either. This way you can make constant progress without getting frustrated or bored repeating the same things you already know.

2. Your own playing should satisfy you to a point that it becomes a positive reinforcement to practising.

3. With something new, try to practise it until you are proficient before moving on. However if something is too hard it's best not to get frustrated, move on to something else. When you come back to it later you'll be better.

Practise doesn't make perfect, perfect practices makes perfect. It's *quality* not so much quantity that counts!

Stretching Exercises

Stretching can enhance performance and protect against injury such as RSI (repetitive strain injury) that can be common for musicians. If you stretch then it stops your muscles and tendons getting stiff later on. With some of the material covered in this book it would be a good idea to stretch a little before and after. Here are some stretches, don't try to do any of them further than you feel is comfortable…

A. Keep both arms straight and stretch them out while using one hand to hold back the fingers of the other. This stretches the wrist flexors.

B. The hand reversed the other way stretches the wrist extensors.

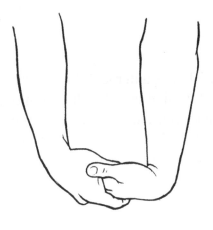

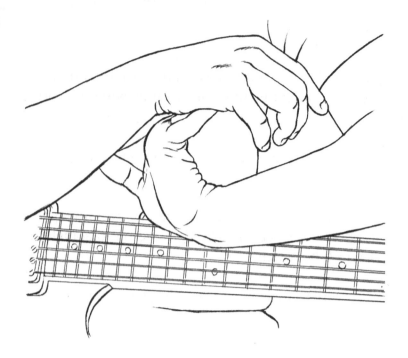

C. If you have the guitar on your lap and want to do a quick stretch, you can easily stretch your hands in front of you.

If you have been sitting with a guitar for a while it can affect your upper back. This is the stiffest area of the back and often becomes even less mobile with a sustained position.

D. Lean backward over the back of a strong enough chair and hold this position for 10 seconds, repeat this 5 times. Putting a rolled up magazine or towel behind your upper back can help. This stretch flexes your back the opposite way that it would have been while playing guitar.

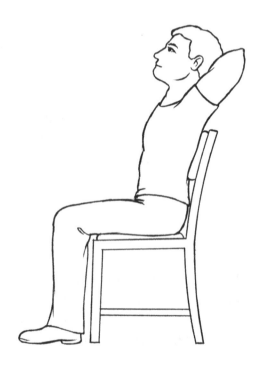

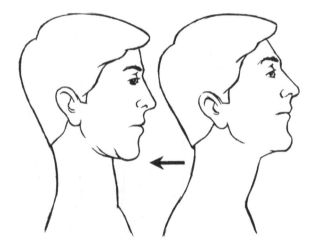

E. This counteracts the forward head posture that can develop in musicians. Tuck your chin in gently and pull your head back gently. This is best done while sitting upright.

G. The following stretch keeps the Median nerve mobile. The Median nerve controls some of the main finger flexors. This stretch is good for playing where more strength is generally needed such as the Bass guitar, which requires more pressure to push down on the frets.

1. Start with your shoulder down and elbow bent with your thumb pointing backwards.

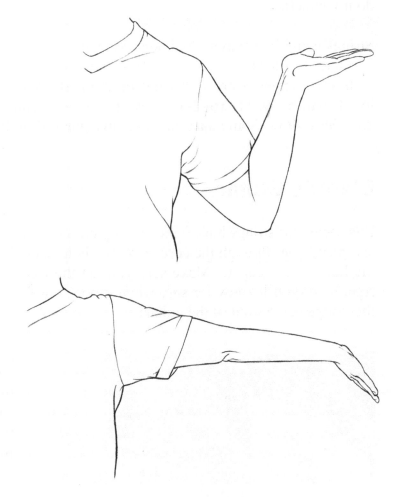

2. Slowly extend your whole arm keeping your shoulder down and wrist bent backward until you can feel reasonable tension in your forearm. Repeat this up to six times.

Qigong balls – two iron balls of about 1.5″ in diameter that you circulate around each other in your palm. You could try it clockwise and counter clockwise, one way will be harder than the other. This flow-like motion of the finger joints with minimum force makes the hand muscles feel smoother and is good for repetitive strain injury. This can also be good for your hand if you use a computer mouse, as are stretches D and E if you sit at a computer.

How to String a Guitar

To string any kind of guitar, for the first time it might be better to get someone who knows how, although if you follow this guide and make sure you are careful you could do it yourself.

Strings come in different thickness (known as *gauges*). The gauge of the high E string is referred to for a set. A set of 9 gauge strings means that the high E string is 0.009 inches in diameter (nine thousands of an inch). A set of 9 gauge strings from high E to low E will be: 9, 11, 16, 24w, 32w, 42w (w = wound), while a set of 10's: 10, 13, 17, 26w, 36w, 46w. Some manufacturers may have slightly different gauge sequences.

Electric Guitar

Electric guitar strings have a metal hoop on one end. The opposite sharp end goes through the corresponding hole behind the bridge at the back of the guitar. Make sure you get the right string for the right hole (you'll know for sure when it pops out from the hole on the bridge at the front of the guitar).

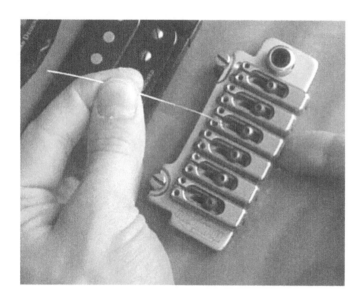

As you gently pull the string through, the hoop at the other end should eventually catch inside the bridge. Make sure the hoop is fully in the bridge and not snagged on something else.

That's the simple bit out of the way. Next the head of the guitar where the tuning pegs are.

Place the end of the string through the hole in the peg. If you wrap the string around the peg before winding it tight you can make sure the string is not wound around the peg too few or too many times before actually tightening it, plus it saves time winding. However, *before we do* there are some important things to consider, explained on the next page…

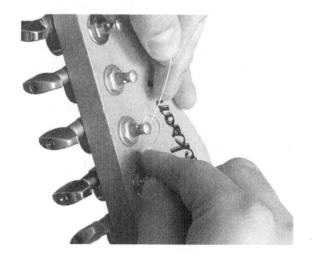

Here is what we are aiming for…

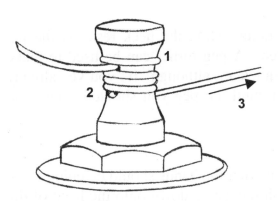

For the first time around the peg the string is wrapped above the hole (1) and from then on downward (2). This way the string overlaps itself making it more secure.

Wrapping it down the rest of the way also increases the angle of the string over the nut making it more secure within it (3).

The strings need to come out on the side of the peg that makes them as straight as possible when looking at the guitar face-on. This is especially important for pegs that are closer to the nut because if the string comes out on the wrong side it will push sideways within the nut and could slip out if played harshly (4).

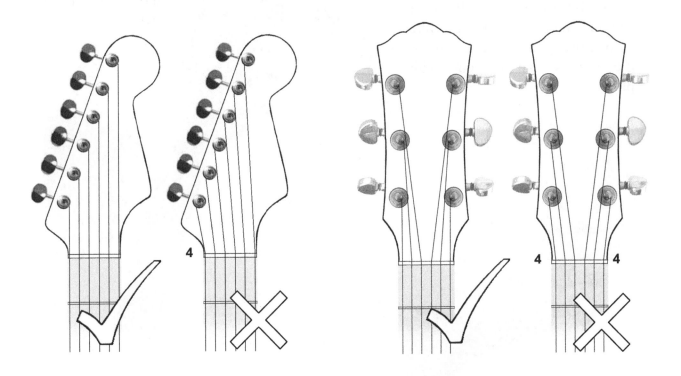

Each of the strings should be wound around the peg at least 3 times. The thicker the string is the less times you can wind it around. The thinner strings can be wound around the peg a few times more, as long as it's not so many it starts to look untidy.

With all this in mind we can wrap the string around the peg (remember; over then under and coming out of the correct side) and start to tighten it. On the next page is how to tighten the peg...

Hold the guitar as follows...

The feet steady the guitar while the neck rests on the leg leaving the hands free. A peg turner can be used to make turning the pegs quicker, although if you've already wrapped the string around the peg you shouldn't have too far to go.

Below is a close up of what the hands should be doing. The thumb is used to push the string down onto the head of the guitar (5) while the fingers pull the string up gently (6) to give it tension so it stays in place around the peg while it is tightened...

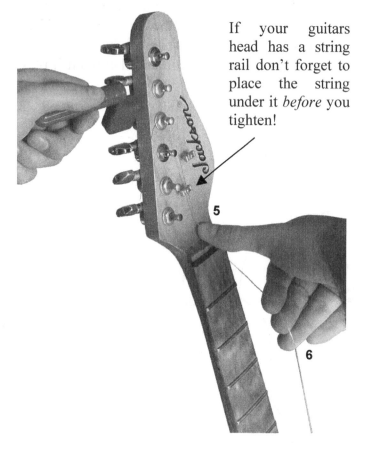

If your guitars head has a string rail don't forget to place the string under it *before* you tighten!

Once the strings are all on it should look something like below, pretty messy! The ends of the strings can be cut with pliers...

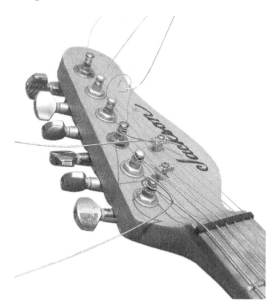

Here's the other head type with the ends of the strings cut. They haven't been cut too short otherwise the stub ends can be sharp and hazardous...

Acoustic Guitar

Acoustic guitar strings have a hoop on one end just like electric guitar strings. For the examples here a twelve-string acoustic is used but the process is the same for a six string.

Take out the bridge pin...

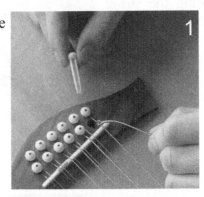

Place the hoop end of the string into the hole as far as it will go...

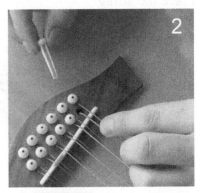

Put the pin back in...

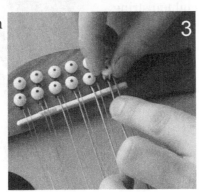

Push down so the string is secure...

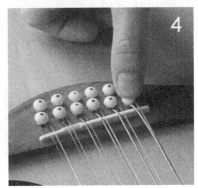

Most acoustic guitars have the same type of head as electric guitars, so the process for attaching the strings to the tuning pegs will be the same.

If not, then it's probably the same as the Classical guitar head (page 127).

Classical Guitar

Classical strings are plain on both ends so it doesn't matter which way round they go but start at the bridge. In the following example the low E string is used...

Place the string into the correct bridge hole...

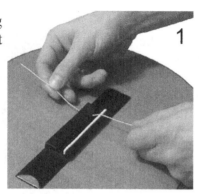

Bring the string around itself then over and under twice...

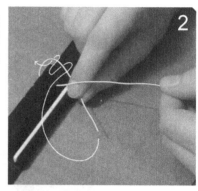

It should look like this...

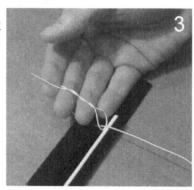

Tighten string...

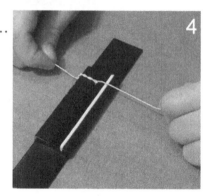

In the example the low E string is wound around itself twice, as should the A and D strings be. For the smaller, smooth strings (G, B and high E) you should loop them around three times to make sure they don't slip out when the string is finally tightened at the tuning peg.

Now onto the other end of the string at the guitars head. There's more over the page on that but in the meantime here's what we are aiming for. The strings should be wound so they come out from above the peg, not underneath. Similar also applies to the classical as the electric and acoustic; make sure the strings come out from the peg in a way that makes them as straight as possible when looking at the guitar face-on. Each of the strings should be wound around the peg at least 3 times, the thicker the string is the less amount of times you can wind it around while the thinner strings can be wound around a few times more.

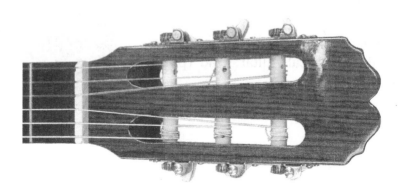

Attach the string to the head as follows…

Pass the string through the peg hole…

1

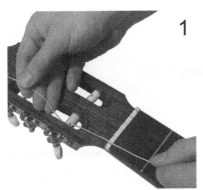

Tie the end around itself once to make it more secure…

2

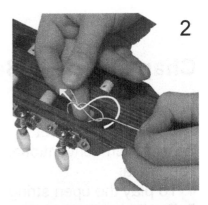

Tighten string…

3

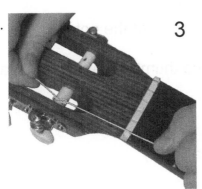

Hold the string as you would an electric guitar (page 124) while turning the peg…

4

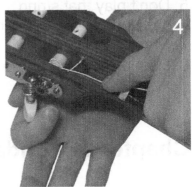

The ends of the strings sticking out from the bridge may cause a buzzing noise when the guitar is played but don't cut them yet because the strings need to settle into place. The guitar will tend to go out of tune (flat) for a couple of days while tension in the strings makes the knots gradually tighten, so it will need to be tuned more regularly for a short period. Once the strings are settled after a couple of days then you can cut the ends off.

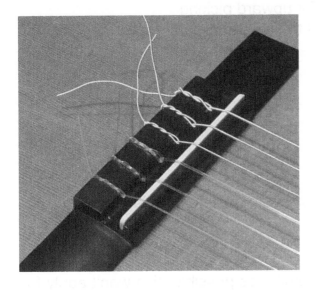

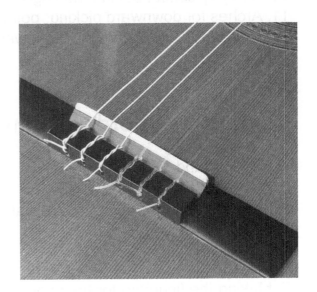

Answers

Chapter 1 - The Beginning (page 20)

1. The B string
2. Just behind the fret
3. To match conventional notation, also it's what you see when looking down at your guitar
4. To play the open string
5. Don't play that string
6. No, they are like a chart that tells us the pitch of the notes
7. Rhythm
8. Rest the wrist / muscle at the base of the thumb area on the guitar

Chapter 2 - Fundamentals (page 36)

1. Enharmonic equivalent
2. Two frets
3. One fret
4. The same note at a higher or lower pitch
5. Tone, Tone, Semitone, Tone, Tone, Tone, Semitone
6. Da Capo (from the head). Go back to the beginning of the piece
7. D
8. G$\sharp$
9. B
10. Roughly central behind the fingers
11. Arches for downward picking, points for upward picking
12. The 3rd, 6th and 7th have been lowered to give the $\flat$3rd, $\flat$6th and $\flat$7th

Chapter 3 - Chords (page 61)

1. Root, 3rd and 5th
2. Root, $\flat$3rd and 5th
3. They are using some of the intervals more than once for a fuller sound
4. D
5. D
6. E
7. Making the fingering for the chords as similar as possible, this won't apply for all chord changes.
8. To stay in time and measure in between to know when to come in when the chords are actually played

Chapter 4 - Playing by Shapes (page 78)

1. Two
2. No
3. Yes
4. The B string
5. From that string upwards the shape needs to be moved up by a fret
6. Root and 5th
7. 5 (so a D power chord for example would be D5)
8. Five notes
9. Root, 2nd, 3rd, 5th, 6th
10. Root, $\flat$3rd, 4th, 5th, $\flat$7th
11. Two octaves

Chapter 5 - Reading Rhythm (page 99)

1. How long a note lasts
2. Four
3. Two
4. How many beats per bar
5. What kind of beat
6. Six eighth note beats per bar
7. An eighth note
8. Two
9. Quarter note rest
10. They are joined together
11. The strongest beats
12. By half
13. A Tie
14. It's a dotted whole note so it would last for six quarter notes (or three half notes)
15. Only one note, the second note extends the length of time the first

Chapter 6 - Further Techniques (page 117)

1. When a finger presses down across multiple strings on the same fret
2. The A string
3. The low E string
4. Drop D
5. Barre across with one finger
6. Palm mute
7. Hammer-on
8. Pull-off
9. It's a slide
10. A semitone bend

Audio created on PC; Athlonx2 3800+ 3.25Gig RAM, through a UX2 (Line 6) into Cubase Essential 5 (Steinberg). Drums programmed using EZ Drummer (Toontrack). Real Band (PG music) used for backing band on tracks 8, 9, 10, 11, 16, 17, 18, 19, 33, 34, 35, 36, 37, 38, 39, 42.

All songs (except for Canon in A, Twinkle Twinkle Little Star, Frere Jacques, Greensleeves, Amazing Grace, Bayou Noir and Florida Blues) composed by Gareth Evans

Guitar played by Gareth Evans on tracks 1, 2, 3, 4, 5, 6, 7, 8, 9, 10, 12, 14, 16, 18, 20, 21, 22, 23, 24, 25, 27, 29, 31, 32, 33, 35, 37, 40, 41.

Bass played by Gareth Evans on tracks 3, 4, 5, 6, 7, 12, 13, 14, 15, 20, 21, 22, 23, 24, 25, 26, 27, 28, 29, 30, 31, 32, 40, 41.

Drums programmed by Gareth Evans on tracks 3, 4, 5, 6, 7, 12, 13, 14, 15, 20, 21, 22, 23, 24, 25, 26, 27, 28, 29, 30, 31, 32, 40, 41.

Lightning Source UK Ltd.
Milton Keynes UK
UKOW07f2044020615

252770UK00006B/116/P